THE MODERATELY MOTIVATED MAN'S GUIDE TO MONEY

REDUCE STRESS AND TAKE CHARGE OF YOUR FINANCES (WITHOUT TRYING TOO HARD)

RICK RESNICK

THE HUSBAND SCHOOL

The Husband School® presents:

The Moderately Motivated Man's Guide to Money:
Reduce Stress and Take Charge of Your Finances
(Without Trying Too Hard)

Note on Authorship and Editorial Process:

This book was developed with the support of modern AI writing and research tools under the author's full creative direction. All final content reflects the author's voice and editorial judgment. Human editors and early readers reviewed the manuscript to ensure clarity and accuracy.

First paperback edition September 2026

First ebook edition September 2026

ISBN 979-8-9912429-8-1 (paperback)

ISBN 979-8-9912429-9-8 (ebook)

www.ModeratelyMotivatedMan.com

ALSO BY RICK RESNICK

The Moderately Motivated Man's Guide to Time Management: Declutter Your Days and Win Back Your Time (Without Trying Too Hard)

The Moderately Motivated Man's Guide to Habits: Start Small and Build What Lasts (Without Trying Too Hard)

The New Husband's Survival Guide: The Secrets to a Happy Marriage While Navigating Sex, Money and a Shared Bathroom

CONTENTS

PREFACE: ABOUT THIS SERIES

WHO IS THE MODERATELY MOTIVATED MAN?

The Moderately Motivated Man is a capable, thoughtful guy trying to manage a full life without turning it into a high-wire act.

He has responsibilities. Deadlines. People who depend on him. He wants to build something meaningful: in his career, relationships, health, and yes, his finances.

But he also wants balance.

He doesn't want to spend every spare minute optimizing spreadsheets or dissecting investment strategies. He doesn't want to treat personal growth like a second job. He wants progress that fits into a real calendar: one that already includes work, family, and the occasional night when he can sit on the couch and do nothing.

He knows he could be sharper in certain areas. He's open to improvement, but he's not interested in extremes.

He's ambitious, not obsessive. Steady, not frantic. Motivated, moderately.

If that sounds familiar, you're in good company.

WHO THIS BOOK IS FOR

This book (and this series) is for regular men with real lives who seek meaningful improvement without becoming self-improvement projects. It's for the guy who wants:

- a financial approach without unnecessary complexity
- an investing strategy without market obsession, and
- peace of mind without constant monitoring

If money has ever felt heavier than it should—not crushing, just persistent—this book was written with you in mind.

THE GUIDE SERIES PROMISE: SMART HELP, WITHOUT THE HYPE

The *Moderately Motivated Man* series exists to help men get better at life without turning personal development into an obsession.

Here, you'll find practical, durable strategies designed to fit into the life you already have, not the fantasy life sold by productivity gurus or finance influencers.

No pressure. No lectures. No overnight transformations. Just solid thinking. Clear structure. And systems that run quietly once they're in place.

Each book focuses on a core area that affects everything else—time, habits, money, health, and more—and makes that area lighter, not heavier.

And each book is intentionally concise. You don't need 600 pages of theory. You need clarity, direction, and a plan you can actually maintain.

Our guiding principle remains simple: Get Better at Life *(Without Trying Too Hard)*.

This installment focuses on money. Why? Because when money feels heavy, it weighs on everything else. When it's structured, automated, and understood, it supports everything else.

Let's build that structure.

INTRODUCTION

TAKE CHARGE OF YOUR FINANCES (WITHOUT TRYING TOO HARD)

At some point, many men realize they understand how to earn money... but aren't entirely sure they understand how money works.

Paychecks make sense. Bills make sense. Saving "for a rainy day" makes sense.

But investing? Retirement math? Asset allocation? Long-term strategy? Those topics often feel like they belong in a different language. Maybe not Flemish or Urdu, but not one you're fluent in, either.

It isn't because you're incapable or irresponsible. It's because no one ever explained the fundamentals in plain English.

The result isn't a disaster. But you feel uncertain. Maybe even uncomfortable. There's a nagging feeling that you are missing out on a key life skill.

You suspect you should be doing something more strategic. You've heard terms such as "index funds" and "compound growth." You know consistency matters, but if someone asked you to explain your long-term money approach clearly, you might not know how to answer.

That inability is common. And it's fixable. I know from experience. At age 30, I couldn't have told you what a mutual fund was. Outside of a very modest 401(k), I had no investment accounts, much less a long-term plan.

Soon thereafter, I became an educated investor. And I began taking charge of my financial future.

For many people, clarity begins with a little guidance. In my case, it began with a book: *The Wealthy Barber.* It wasn't flashy. It didn't promise shortcuts. It told a straightforward story about an ordinary man who built significant wealth through ordinary behavior:

- Live below your means.
- Invest consistently.
- Keep costs low.
- Let compounding do its quiet work.

There were no tricks, predictions, financial heroics—or hot stock tips from Uncle Ernie.

That framework was liberating. It stripped money of mystery. It showed that wealth wasn't about brilliance; it was about structure and patience. The week I finished the book, I went to the investment firm in the lobby of my office building and handed them a $500 check.

My new financial journey had begun. Decades later, I'm still pleasantly surprised by how well it worked out.

Understanding the principles is one thing, but living them calmly over decades is another.

The Wealthy Barber explained what to do. Real life challenges you to keep doing it, through market drops, noisy headlines, career changes, and the temptation to tinker when things feel uncertain.

That's where *The Moderately Motivated Man's Guide to Money* enters the conversation.

WHAT THIS BOOK IS (AND WHAT IT ISN'T)

This is not a traditional personal finance manual. We are not going to calculate optimal portfolio weights, debate sector allocations, hand out stock picks, or explore tax loopholes.

There are excellent resources and professionals who specialize in those details.

This book focuses on something more foundational: your approach to money. Because most financial stress doesn't come from choosing between Fund A and Fund B. It comes from a lack of clarity.

Not knowing exactly where you stand. Not knowing whether your approach is actually working. Not knowing whether you're falling behind.

When money feels undefined, it becomes intimidating. And when something feels intimidating, we either obsess over it or avoid it. Neither response builds confidence.

What instills confidence is structure, which can include the following:

- a simple savings rhythm
- a diversified investment approach
- clear long-term thinking
- defined boundaries around lifestyle stretch
- the ability to stay steady when markets wobble

That's what we're building here.

WHY MINDSET MATTERS MORE THAN MECHANICS

The mechanics of investing matter, but they matter less than most people think.

Financial success is rarely about finding the perfect fund. It's about behavior.

Can you invest consistently when markets are boring? Can you keep investing when markets are scary? Can you define "enough" before your expenses define it for you? Can you resist comparison when others appear to be sprinting ahead?

Those are mindset questions, not technical ones.

You don't need to become a financial expert. You need a reliable money operating system, one that runs quietly in the background and keeps you from making emotional decisions at the worst possible times.

That's what this book is designed to provide.

WHAT YOU'LL LEARN HERE

Over the next 10 chapters, you'll learn how to do the following:

- Reduce vagueness and understand where you stand.
- Build breathing room instead of pressure.
- Create a simple savings rhythm that runs automatically.
- Invest steadily without turning it into a sport.
- Plan for the long term without panic.

- Stay the course when others wobble.
- Define "enough" on your own terms.
- Keep your system simple, even as your life grows more complex.

None of this requires extreme effort. It requires decisions made calmly, implemented cleanly, and repeated over time.

You don't need brilliance. You need a simple structure.

At some point, you will likely open an account. Or adjust one. Or speak with a professional. Or automate contributions into a low-cost, diversified fund.

When you do, the mechanics will matter. But here's the key: Those mechanics are far easier to execute when you already understand the philosophy behind them.

You know why you're investing. You know what role money plays in your life. And, you've defined your version of "enough."

Without that foundation, the technical details feel overwhelming. With it, they feel procedural.

The goal of this book is to help you build that foundation.

THE BIGGER PICTURE

This is the third book in the *Moderately Motivated Man* series for a reason.

Time shapes your days. Habits shape your behavior. Money shapes your options. Get those three aligned, and life becomes noticeably steadier.

Not perfect. Not immune to uncertainty. But grounded.

You don't need to retire early to benefit from a calm

money approach. You don't need a seven-figure portfolio to feel secure. You don't need to "win" at finance.

You need to understand it well enough that it stops feeling mysterious. You need to design a system that works. You need to be able to look at your financial life and think, "This makes sense."

That's success.

If you're ready to think about money clearly, move from confusion to confidence, and let go of "winging it," then turn the page.

It's time to reduce stress and take charge of your finances, because success doesn't have to be stressful.

CHAPTER 1
LIGHTEN THE LOAD

CHAPTER SUMMARY

Money often feels heavier than it should. Not because you're doing something wrong, but because things are unclear, and that creates anxiety. This chapter explains why avoidance is a normal stress response and how uncertainty erodes confidence. Instead of jumping straight to tactics, we begin by clearing the fog. We separate your identity from your numbers, and we turn emotion into something you can actually work with. When you replace ambiguity with clarity, the weight starts to lift. Financial peace isn't about pushing harder. It's about knowing where you stand.

SECTION 1: WHY MONEY FEELS HEAVY

THE WEIGHT OF NOT KNOWING

When you really think about it, money is just numbers.

It's digits on a screen. A few lines on a statement. A

direct deposit every two weeks. A bill that arrives in an envelope or an inbox.

There's nothing physically heavy about it. Yet, for a lot of us, money feels heavy.

Not dramatic. Not catastrophic. Just... heavy.

It sits in the background of your life like a low-grade hum. You don't always notice it, but it's there when you make decisions. When you swipe your card. When you think about changing jobs. When your kid talks about college. It's there when the car starts making an expensive-sounding noise.

Most money stress doesn't come from being bad with money. It comes from not knowing exactly where you stand and worrying that one wrong move, one surprise bill, or one bad month could knock everything sideways.

That uncertainty weighs on us, so we tend to avoid making money decisions. We're not lazy or irresponsible; uncertainty is uncomfortable.

AVOIDANCE IS A STRESS RESPONSE

If you've ever let a bank statement or an invoice sit unopened on the counter for a day or two, you know this feeling. If you've ever told yourself, "I'll check the accounts this weekend," only to find the weekend has passed, you know this feeling.

Avoidance is not a character flaw. It's a stress response. Your brain doesn't enjoy ambiguity. It especially doesn't like ambiguity tied to survival, status, and security—which is what money represents, whether we like it or not.

Instead of leaning in, we subtly lean away. We don't look too closely. We don't run the numbers. We don't ask the big questions.

THE UNCERTAINTY LOOP

Ironically, the less we look at a money-related task, the heavier it feels. The heavier it feels, the less we look.

That loop is where most money stress lives.

The Moderately Motivated Man doesn't need a lecture about discipline. He needs relief from that loop. Because here's the truth: you can be intelligent, hardworking, and responsible ... and still feel uneasy about money.

You can have a decent income and still feel like you're behind. You can have savings and still feel exposed. You can be doing "fine" on paper and still feel like you're one step from chaos.

That doesn't make you unusual. It makes you human.

A lot of traditional money advice skips this part. It jumps straight to tactics such as budgeting harder, investing more, cutting expenses, maximizing this, or optimizing that.

But tactics layered on top of anxiety just create more pressure. If money already feels heavy, the last thing you need is someone yelling at you to lift more.

What you need is to understand why it feels heavy in the first place.

Here's when money weighs you down:

- You don't know your real monthly burn rate.
- You're unsure how much wiggle room you actually have.
- You don't know what would happen if income were to stop for three months.
- You're vaguely aware that investing is important but unsure if you're doing it right.

- You carry old money assumptions from childhood, mistakes, or setbacks.

None of that should create panic, but all of it can shake your confidence.

CONFIDENCE IS KEY

Confidence is the real currency here. When you lack clarity, you lack confidence. When you lack confidence, you hesitate. When you hesitate, you fall behind.

But this is just a system problem. And it can be fixed.

This book is not about becoming obsessed with money. It's about removing the uncertainty that creates unnecessary weight.

Something subtle yet powerful happens when you finally understand your financial picture:

- What's coming in
- What's going out
- What your basic safety cushion looks like
- What your long-term path is

At that point, money loses its power to intimidate. You stop reacting. You stop second-guessing. You stop feeling like you're constantly "catching up."

From there, something important happens. Confidence changes behavior. Behavior creates consistency. Consistency—not genius, hustle, or obsession—often creates long-term financial success.

That's the formula we'll be discussing here.

It's not about relentless effort, spreadsheets at

midnight, or chasing the hottest investment trend—just clarity, confidence, and steady repetition.

The goal isn't to conquer money. The goal is to make it mundane, so it feels lighter.

And light money doesn't run your life. It supports it.

SECTION 2: YOU'RE NOT BEHIND. YOU'RE UNCLEAR

COMPARISON DISTORTS REALITY

There's a particular kind of anxiety that comes from the statement, "I should be further along."

Further along compared to whom? Based on what timeline? Measured against which benchmark?

Money is uniquely good at triggering comparison. Your friend bought a bigger house. Someone at work just got a raise. Your neighbor seems to renovate something every six months. Social media assures you that everyone else has mastered investing, real estate, side businesses, and international travel by age 32.

It's easy to internalize the message: I'm late. But here's what most people won't tell you: A surprising number of those same people feel exactly the same way.

HIDDEN STRAIN IS COMMON

Financial insecurity can be subtle. Debt can be hard to see, and lifestyle stretch doesn't always show up on the surface. Even people with real wealth can feel unsure about their future.

The issue isn't usually that you're far behind. It's that

you don't have a clear, grounded picture of where you actually are.

Uncertainty makes you second-guess everything. Clarity builds confidence.

Imagine two guys earning the same income:

One has no idea what his monthly expenses truly are, vaguely guesses at his savings, and checks his accounts only when forced.

The other knows his core monthly costs, has a simple savings rhythm in place, and steadily contributes to his investments.

Same income. Same potential. Different experiences.

The second man sleeps better, not because he's richer but because he's clearer.

NUMBERS ARE NOT IDENTITY

Clarity is powerful. It enables you to begin separating your identity from your finances.

Your bank balance doesn't define you. Your net worth does not equal your personal worth. Your past financial mistakes don't reflect your intelligence.

They are data points. That's all.

You should be able to look at the numbers without turning them into a morale-crushing performance review.

You are not "bad with money." You probably just need a system.

LABELING THE LIGHTS

Think about this: If your car dashboard showed only random blinking lights with no labels, driving would feel stressful. Even if the car were functioning perfectly, the lack of information would make every mile tense.

Money works the same way. Unlabeled lights create anxiety. Even if everything is fine, it doesn't feel fine—and you're still reaching for the antacids.

This chapter is about labeling the lights. You don't need perfection. You don't need mastery or a 42-tab spreadsheet. You just need to know where you stand.

Knowing where you stand is often surprisingly anticlimactic. You look. You calculate. You realize, "Oh. That's it?"

Sometimes the numbers are better than you feared. Sometimes they're tighter than you'd like.

Either way, they're visible. And visible is better than vague.

Once the numbers are visible, you can begin to make calm adjustments. That's when the weight starts to lift.

SECTION 3: THE CALM PATH FORWARD

A QUIET FINANCIAL OPERATING SYSTEM

Before we talk about tactics—like budgets, investing, emergency buffers, and automation—we need to make a key point: This is not a book about extreme actions.

It's not about saving half your income, cutting every pleasure, timing markets, or lowering your taxes. There are other books for that.

This book is about building a calm, simple way to run your money—one that reduces the unknowns, gives you some breathing room, keeps investing straightforward, helps you spend with intention, and lets things run in the background.

To do that, we are going to cover the following:

- How to know where you stand, without panic
- How to spend in a way that aligns with your life, not someone else's
- How to build a simple plan, not a complicated one
- How to invest without obsessing
- How to protect what you build
- How to stay steady when life gets noisy

Notice what's missing: No hustle mandate. No guilt. No shame. No comparisons with your peers.

SIMPLE BEATS IMPRESSIVE

One of the most life-changing financial concepts is deceptively simple: Anyone can do this. Not just financial wizards. Not just CEOs. Not just people born into money. Anyone.

Here are the basics: Live below your means. Invest consistently. Let time and compounding do their quiet work. Avoid drama. Repeat.

Does it work every time? Is it a guarantee for success? No, and no. But it has worked for countless people for generations.

CONSISTENCY OVER CLEVERNESS

The compounding of money is not flashy. It's about patience that rewards consistency more than cleverness.

Delayed gratification is not a sacrifice. You simply trade a little comfort now for a lot of stability later.

Living below your means is not punishment. It's how you create breathing room, or "margin." And margin creates peace of mind.

Instead of intensity, all that's needed is clarity, confidence, and consistency. Before you know it, money will feel lighter and a lot less stressful.

LET MONEY RUN IN THE BACKGROUND

By the end of this book, we don't want you to feel fired up. We want you to feel steady.

You don't need to think, "I'm going to crush it." More like, "Okay. I see it now. I've got this."

Money should not dominate your mental space. It should support your life quietly. It should fund your home, time, relationships, and experiences, without constantly demanding attention.

That is what a calm money life looks like. And it starts here, without a massive overhaul or a vow to change everything. It starts with replacing uncertainty with clarity. It starts with knowing you are not broken, behind, or incapable.

You are simply one clear system away from being confident with your money. Let's fix that.

KEY TAKEAWAYS FROM CHAPTER 1

1. *Why Money Feels Heavy.* Money feels heavy when it's vague. Uncertainty triggers avoidance, and avoidance erodes confidence. That loop creates stress. Clarity reduces the weight.

2. *You're Not Behind. You're Unclear.* Most financial anxiety comes from comparison and incomplete information, not actual failure. Your numbers are data, not identity. When you see them clearly, insecurity starts to fade.
3. *The Calm Path Forward.* Financial peace comes from simple, steady systems, not intensity or brilliance. Live below your means, invest consistently, avoid drama, and let time do the heavy lifting.

ACKNOWLEDGMENTS

This chapter reflects the behavioral lens through which modern personal finance is increasingly viewed: that money stress is often psychological before it is mathematical. The emphasis on identity, uncertainty, and temperament aligns with themes explored in Morgan Housel's *The Psychology of Money*, particularly the idea that how we feel about money often matters more than how much we know about it.

MODERATELY PAINLESS EXERCISE

THE THREE-NUMBER SNAPSHOT

If money feels heavy, it's usually because it's blurry. So let's make it slightly less blurry.

This will take 10–15 minutes. No spreadsheets. No perfection.

Open your banking and brokerage apps, or log in on your laptop. (If you manage money jointly with a spouse or partner, use your combined household numbers throughout this exercise.) Write down three numbers:

1. Total Liquid Assets. Add up checking, savings, money market accounts, and taxable brokerage accounts. (But not retirement accounts.) Include anything you could reasonably access within a few days without penalties.
2. Total Debt. Include mortgage balance, car loans, student loans, credit card balances, and personal loans. Round if you'd like. This is clarity, not accounting.
3. Monthly Take-Home Income. Use your net pay: what actually hits your bank account in a typical month. If income varies, use a recent average.

That's it. Pause. Look at the three numbers together. Then write one honest sentence:

"Seeing these numbers makes me feel _____."

Relieved? Behind? More in control than expected? A little exposed?

There is no right reaction. The point is visibility. Vagueness creates weight. Specifics reduce it, even if the specifics aren't perfect.

You are not fixing anything today. You are simply understanding where you are.

Close the apps. That's enough for now. Done.

CHAPTER 2
KNOW WHERE YOU STAND

CHAPTER SUMMARY

Most financial stress doesn't come from big mistakes; it comes from uncertainty. In this chapter, you'll learn how to face your numbers without drama, map your cash flow in simple terms, and create visibility around your net worth and margin of safety. None of this requires spreadsheets at midnight or a personality transplant. It requires calm awareness. When you stop avoiding and start observing, money shifts from a source of anxiety to a system you can adjust—and that's where confidence begins.

SECTION 1: FACE THE NUMBERS WITHOUT DRAMA

THE MOMENT OF DECISION

There's a moment that many people stress over. It's not

dramatic. It doesn't involve alarms or flashing lights. It's usually just you, your phone, and a banking app.

You open it. Or you don't.

That tiny decision—"Do I look or delay?"—is where a lot of financial stress lives.

Most avoidance is subtle. It sounds like this: "I'll check it later." "Next week I'll really sit down with it." "I should probably organize my sock drawer first." Really, any excuse will do.

The problem isn't that you don't care. It's that you care enough for it to feel uncomfortable.

Money carries an emotional weight. It represents security. Freedom. Competence. Stability. So when the numbers feel uncertain, your brain treats that uncertainty like potential danger.

And what does your brain do with potential danger? It scans. It worries. Or it avoids.

RELIEF NOW, TENSION LATER

Avoidance feels safer in the short term, but it makes you feel more tense over time. The less you look, the more your imagination fills in the gaps. The more your imagination fills in the gaps, the more stressed you feel.

Chapter 1 discussed lightening the emotional load. This chapter focuses on the simplest, calmest way to keep that load from building back up: Look at the numbers.

Not dramatically. Not judgmentally. Not with a vow to change your life overnight. Just look.

SEPARATE DATA FROM IDENTITY

The Moderately Motivated Man does not storm into his

finances like he's raiding a castle. He walks in like a homeowner checking the thermostat. It's about data, not judgment.

That phrase matters. When you step on a scale, it gives you a number. It doesn't call you lazy. It doesn't tell you you've failed. It doesn't predict your future. It just reports.

Your bank accounts do the same thing. If your balance is lower than you expected, that is information. If your credit card balance is higher than you'd like, that is information. If your savings are stronger than you realized, that is also information.

The emotional charge comes from the story *you* attach to it. "I should have known better." "I always mess this up." "I'm terrible with money."

That story isn't necessary. Numbers don't need narrative.

There's a powerful shift that happens when you decide that looking is normal. Not heroic. Not brave. Just normal.

You check your accounts the way you check the weather. You don't take it personally. You don't yell at the clouds. You just observe the conditions and dress accordingly.

Facing the numbers without drama means you stop turning every glance into a referendum on your character.

FIVE MINUTES IS ENOUGH

It also means you shrink the task. One of the reasons financial check-ins can feel overwhelming is because we imagine a marathon session: spreadsheets, calculators, life reevaluations, perhaps a cup of black coffee, and a solemn vow to "be better."

That's not required. The first step is five minutes. Open

the accounts. Look at the balances. Notice what's pending. Close the app.

That's it.

You are not solving your retirement in one sitting. You are building familiarity, which reduces fear.

Think about anything new you've learned in your life, like driving, cooking, or using a new piece of software. The first time feels awkward. The 10th feels manageable. The 50th feels automatic.

Money can work the same way. If you haven't been looking consistently at your accounts, it will feel slightly uncomfortable at first. That doesn't mean something is wrong. It means you're building a new habit of awareness.

There is something surprisingly calming about knowing exactly where you stand, even if where you stand isn't perfect.

When you can look at your numbers without your heart rate increasing, you've already made progress. You've broken the avoidance loop.

Once you do that, your confidence can begin to grow.

SECTION 2: MAP YOUR CASH FLOW

TWO SIMPLE QUESTIONS

After you've faced the numbers without drama, the next step is even simpler, though it sounds more technical than it is: Map your cash flow.

That action item can scare people. It sounds like it involves spreadsheets, accounting classes, and an entire weekend of calculations.

Relax. To map your cash flow, you answer two basic questions:

- What's coming in?
- What's going out?

That's it.

INCOME: WHAT'S COMING IN

Start with income. How much money hits your account each month, on average?

If you're salaried, that number is probably predictable. If your income comes from commissions, freelance work, or other variable sources, it might fluctuate. That's fine. You're not looking for perfect precision. You're looking for a realistic average.

Take the last three to six months and calculate a rough monthly average. You're not trying to impress someone or build a ten-year forecast. Just to know.

EXPENSES: WHAT'S GOING OUT

Then move to the other side of the equation. What's going out?

Again, we're not building a forensic audit of every coffee purchase. We're identifying patterns.

Broad categories include housing, transportation, food, insurance, utilities, subscriptions, debt payments, savings, and lifestyle spending.

You don't need to track every grocery item or categorize every Amazon order with surgical precision. The goal is clarity, not control.

When you lay it out, even roughly, something interesting happens. The mystery disappears.

You might discover your monthly baseline spending is lower than you feared. Or, maybe it's higher than you assumed. Either way, you've replaced guessing with reality.

Reality is easier to work with than assumptions.

FIND THE FLEX POINTS

This is also where fixed versus variable expenses come into play.

Fixed expenses are predictable: rent, mortgage, insurance, phone bill, and car payment. Variable expenses fluctuate: groceries, dining out, gas, and entertainment.

When you separate these two, you begin to see where flexibility exists. That's powerful.

If your fixed expenses are extremely high relative to your income, that points to how your finances are set up. If your variable spending is the area creeping upward, that tells you something about your behavior.

Neither is a moral issue. They're signals.

Mapping cash flow isn't judgmental. It's about understanding where you stand.

You may realize that your income comfortably covers your essentials, but lifestyle spending quickly absorbs the rest. Or you may notice that you're saving more than you thought, just not intentionally.

Many people feel behind, not because they are financially doomed but because they've never seen the full picture. When you see it, even in rough form, you regain perspective.

KNOW YOUR BURN RATE

You also begin to identify your monthly "burn rate." How much does it cost to live your current life?

Not ideally. Not someday. Right now.

Knowing your burn rate does something subtle but important: It reduces uncertainty. (Notice the pattern?)

If you lost your job tomorrow, how many months could you float? If income dipped temporarily, how tight would things get?

You don't need to panic. You just need to be aware.

A man who knows his monthly costs walks through life differently than a man who doesn't. Instead of feeling anxious, he feels confident because uncertainty shrinks when numbers are visible.

PLAYING THE LONG GAME

This is also where delayed gratification begins to show up.

When you clearly see your cash flow, you can make informed choices. Living below your means stops being a slogan and becomes a visible choice.

If you earn $6,000 a month after taxes and spend $5,500, you're technically afloat. But you're tight. If you earn $6,000 and spend $4,800, you have some breathing room. And that margin creates calm.

You don't have to save half your income. You don't have to follow someone else's aggressive blueprint. But when you see your numbers, you can decide what "below your means" looks like for you.

And once you have even a modest gap between income and expenses, something powerful happens: You can direct that "extra money" toward savings, debt reduction, investing, or your future freedom.

Once you map what's coming in and what's going out, money stops being an abstract force and becomes a system you can adjust.

SECTION 3: CREATE FINANCIAL VISIBILITY

NET WORTH IS A SNAPSHOT

Now we move from monthly cash flow to the bigger picture: net worth.

If cash flow is the rhythm of your financial life, net worth is the snapshot. This is where some people tense up.

"Net worth" sounds intimidating. It sounds like something for wealthy executives or personal finance nerds who look forward to their monthly statements.

In reality, net worth is simple. It's what you own, minus what you owe. That's it.

First, add up your assets: checking, savings, investments, retirement accounts, and home equity if you want to include it. Then subtract your liabilities: credit cards, loans, mortgage, and anything outstanding. The result is your net worth.

Don't think of the number as a verdict. It is a snapshot or starting point.

For some readers, that number will be positive. For others, especially if student loans or mortgages are involved, it might be negative. That does not define you. It describes your current position, which can change.

There is something incredibly grounding about writing down that number. Money becomes less about emotion and more about math. You don't need to track it often. Once or twice a year is enough.

ORIENTATION REDUCES ANXIETY

If you were hiking and had no idea which direction you were heading, your anxiety would rise quickly. The moment you see the map and locate yourself, your pulse slows. Financial visibility works the same way. Cash flow shows you the movement. Net worth shows you the direction.

And then there's the margin of safety, one of the most calming concepts in personal finance. It simply means building breathing space between you and chaos.

That buffer might be an emergency fund. It might be a certain level of savings. It might be a low debt-to-income ratio. It's the difference between worrying, "I hope nothing goes wrong," and thinking, "If something goes wrong, I can handle it."

You don't need a mountain of cash to feel secure. Even setting aside a few months' expenses can dramatically reduce stress.

STABILITY FUELS CONSISTENCY

When you combine visibility (your net worth) with margin (your buffer), you create something more valuable than high income on its own: stability.

Stability increases your confidence. Confidence helps you become more consistent with your money. Consistency over time enables your money to compound. This is where the long-term power begins to show up.

(We will dig into the wonders of compounding in

Chapter 5. For now, just understand that compounding is the phenomenon in which your money grows, almost on its own, like a snowball running downhill.)

Compounding is not flashy. It builds over time. If you consistently invest each month in a broad market fund, it doesn't feel dramatic in year one. In year two, it still feels modest. But give it 10 years. Fifteen. Twenty. Time becomes your ally.

But time only works if you stay invested and stay consistent. That's why getting clear now matters so much.

When you know your numbers, you're less likely to panic. When markets dip, you're less likely to make emotional decisions. When headlines scream, you're less likely to abandon your plan.

Knowing your numbers anchors you. It reminds you: this is my system. This is my timeline. This is *my* game. Not your neighbor's. Not your coworker's. Not the loudest voice online. Yours.

This clarity doesn't give you instant wealth or perfect foresight. It gives you calm.

Calm means you can focus on your work without a constant low-level hum of anxiety. Calm means you can enjoy a purchase without wondering whether you've sabotaged your future. Calm means you can make decisions deliberately instead of reactively.

When you know where you stand, you stop guessing. When you stop guessing, progress becomes almost automatic.

LET TIME DO ITS WORK

The Moderately Motivated Man doesn't obsess over his

net worth daily. He doesn't micromanage every market fluctuation. He knows where he stands. He knows his burn rate. He has a buffer. He invests consistently. He lets time work.

And then he goes back to living his life.

That's the point.

Money is not the center. It is support.

This chapter is not about becoming hyper-aware to the point of stress. It's about becoming aware enough to feel grounded.

You've faced the numbers without drama. You've mapped your cash flow. You've created visibility.

From here, we can begin to make intentional choices about spending, saving, investing, and building a system that runs quietly in the background.

But none of that works without this step. You can't adjust what you can't see. Now you can see it.

And that alone takes away much of money's weight.

KEY TAKEAWAYS FROM CHAPTER 2

1. *Face the Numbers Without Drama.* Avoidance makes you feel more anxious. Looking at your accounts calmly and regularly turns money from an emotional trigger into neutral data. Awareness is the first step toward control.
2. *Map Your Cash Flow.* When you know what's coming in, what's going out, and what your monthly burn rate really is, you don't have to guess anymore. You can see your gap and decide what to do about it.

3. *Create Financial Visibility.* Net worth is a snapshot, not a verdict. Along with a margin of safety, it helps you know where you are today. When you can see your position clearly, long-term consistency becomes far easier.

ACKNOWLEDGMENTS

This chapter builds on long-standing principles in personal finance and behavioral economics: that visibility reduces anxiety, that regular check-ins beat dramatic overhauls, and that building a margin of safety creates stability. The concept of a financial "margin of safety," popularized in modern investing by Benjamin Graham and later embraced by long-term investors, reinforces a simple idea: Give yourself some breathing room.

MODERATELY PAINLESS EXERCISE

YOUR SLEEP-WELL-AT-NIGHT NUMBER

Now that you've faced your numbers without drama and mapped your cash flow, let's add one stabilizing layer: margin. This is not a full financial plan. It's a grounding number.

You'll need 10–15 minutes. That's it.

Step 1: Identify Your Core Monthly Burn Rate

On a sheet of paper (or in your Notes app), record your bare-minimum monthly expenses. Not your ideal lifestyle.

Not your "fun month." Just what it costs to keep life running.

Include things like these: housing (rent or mortgage), utilities, groceries (realistic, not aspirational), insurance, transportation, minimum debt payments, and essential subscriptions (Internet, phone, etc.).

Don't chase precision. Round if you need to. You're simply getting clear, not preparing for an audit.

When you're done, you have a rough number: "It costs me about $____ per month to live."

That's your core burn rate.

Step 2: Multiply by Three

Take that monthly number and multiply it by three. That's your Sleep-Well-At-Night (SWAN) number.

Why three? Because three months of core expenses are often enough to turn a potential crisis into a manageable disruption. It creates breathing room. It lowers the pulse.

This is not a rule carved in stone. It's a stabilizing baseline.

Step 3: Compare (Without Judgment)

Now glance at your current liquid savings: checking, savings, money market accounts, and accessible brokerage cash. (You can use your Total Liquid Assets number from Chapter 1.) Are you above the SWAN number? Below it? Right around it?

If you're below it, you're not a failure. You can use it as a direction. If you're above it, you have a great foundation.

When you know your burn rate and your buffer target, uncertainty shrinks. You're no longer thinking, "What if something happens?" You're thinking, "If something happens, here's what I have."

That shift, from uncertainty to clarity, is where calm begins. You're not building a fortress today. You're installing a floor.

Once you know the number, you can gradually build toward it. Quietly. Consistently. Calmly.

CHAPTER 3
SPEND WITH INTENTION

CHAPTER SUMMARY

In this chapter, you'll explore why most spending is reactive—shaped by lifestyle creep, comparison, convenience, and temporary emotion rather than clear intention. You'll see how small, reasonable upgrades can inflate your baseline spending and erode margin over time. Then you'll define what "enough" actually means for your life by separating "being rich" from "building wealth," and by learning how margin (not status) creates flexibility and peace. Finally, you'll build a friction-free spending system with guardrails that protect your priorities automatically, so your money supports your values instead of chasing impulses.

SECTION 1: WHY MOST SPENDING IS REACTIVE

THE SPENDING TRAIL

Most people don't have a spending plan. They have a spending *trail.*

A trail of transactions that made sense in the moment. A dinner here. A subscription there. An upgrade that felt reasonable. A "we deserve it" weekend. An Amazon order at 10:47 p.m. that leaves you with a dedicated hot dog toaster you'll use exactly once.

None of this makes you reckless. It makes you human.

The problem isn't that we spend. The problem is that most of our day-to-day spending is reactive. It responds to stress, comparison, convenience, advertising, temporary emotion, and lifestyle creep.

Rarely does it respond to intention—spending on purpose instead of reacting in the moment.

LIFESTYLE RISES QUIETLY

Let's start with lifestyle creep. It is very subtle. It doesn't arrive like a villain. It arrives like a reward: You get a raise. You upgrade the car. You move to a slightly nicer neighborhood. You start ordering the better bottle of wine. You justify a few more recurring subscriptions because, after all, you work hard.

Individually, each choice feels reasonable. Collectively, they become your new baseline.

What used to feel like a luxury becomes normal. What used to feel like "doing well" becomes "just getting by." That's lifestyle creep.

It's not evil. It's natural.

Humans adapt quickly. What felt exciting last year feels standard today. But here's the hidden cost: When lifestyle rises as quickly as income, margin disappears. And when that breathing room disappears, stress returns.

You can make more money and still feel the same financial pressure. That's not because you're failing. It's because reactive upgrades replaced intentional design.

COMPARISON AND MOOD SPENDING

Then there's social comparison. Money and comparison are lifelong roommates: Your friend buys a bigger house. Your colleague leases a nicer car. Your neighbor remodels their kitchen. Someone on social media seems to be on vacation every month.

Even if you tell yourself it doesn't matter, your brain notices. And it asks, "Should we be doing that, too?"

This is where spending becomes identity-driven instead of value-driven. You're no longer asking, "Do I want this?" You're asking, "Is this what someone like me should have?"

That's a dangerous shift. Once spending becomes about status or signaling, it never ends. There is always someone with more. There is always someone renovating something. There is always someone posting their photos from a better-looking beach.

If your financial life is built around keeping up, you will never arrive.

Which brings us to emotional spending. We don't like to admit it, but money is one of the fastest mood regulators available. Bad day? Order something. Bored? Scroll and click. Stressed? Upgrade something. Celebrating? Spend big.

The purchase gives you a quick hit of relief or excitement.

In truth, most emotional purchases aren't about the item. They're about the feeling, and feelings fade.

The package arrives. You open it. For about 48 hours,

it's your new favorite thing. After that, it disappears onto that shelf in the garage, next to the portable Bluetooth karaoke machine.

The card bill, however, lingers.

Again, this isn't about shame. It's about awareness.

ALIGNMENT RESTORES CONTROL

Reactive spending creates three long-term problems:

1. It inflates your baseline lifestyle.
2. It reduces your financial margin.
3. It disconnects your money from your true values.

When money is disconnected from values, it feels scattered, which weakens confidence. This is why some people earn solid incomes and still feel financially uneasy. It's not that they don't make enough. It's that their money isn't aligned.

The Moderately Motivated Man aims to shift from reaction to intention. When spending becomes intentional, you stop leaking money in directions you don't care about.

More importantly, you start directing money toward the life you actually want—by design.

SECTION 2: DEFINE ENOUGH

THE MISSING WORD

There's a word that almost never appears in modern money conversations: "enough."

Not "more." Not "maximize." Not "optimize." Not "scale."

Enough.

If you never define *enough*, you will chase more forever. And that is exhausting.

One of the most useful distinctions in personal finance is the difference between being rich and having wealth. *Rich* often means high income. *Wealth* means having assets you don't need to spend.

Rich buys the bigger house. Wealth builds flexibility. Rich looks impressive. Wealth sleeps well.

That distinction matters. If your goal is to look rich, you will spend to impress. If your goal is to build wealth, you will spend, save, and invest strategically for your future.

Defining *enough* is where this begins. Enough is not a number someone else gives you. It's a design choice. Enough might mean one or more of these:

- A home you like but don't stretch for
- A car that works but doesn't impress strangers
- Vacations you can pay for without stress
- Savings that let you sleep at night
- Freedom to say no to work you don't want

CHOOSE WHAT TRULY MATTERS

Enough is personal. It forces you to ask yourself, "What does a good life truly look like for me?"

Not for your neighbor. Not for your college roommate. Not for social media. For you.

Most men skip this question. They jump straight to tactics: invest more, earn more, or upgrade more. But if you don't know what you're building toward, you'll keep building indefinitely.

Let's slow this down. What are your real priorities? Time with family? Travel? A paid-off house? Early retirement? Flexible work? Security for your kids? The ability to care for aging parents?

Now ask a harder question: "What do you not care about as much as you think you should?"

This is where spending becomes powerful. When you clearly define what matters, you give yourself permission to ignore the rest.

Maybe you don't care about designer clothes, luxury cars, having a massive house, or keeping up with the neighbors.

That clarity is freeing. You stop spending to impress. You start spending to support. And when you support what matters, money feels lighter once again.

There's also something kind of radical about deciding you don't need infinite growth. You lessen the pressure.

If your lifestyle is constantly stretching to match potential income, you're always on a treadmill. Defining enough gives you a stopping point. It allows you to say, "This is sufficient." And that creates peace of mind.

Delayed gratification fits naturally here. Delayed gratification is often misunderstood as self-denial. It's not. It's choosing long-term strength over short-term impulse. It's saying:

- "I could upgrade now, but I'd rather build margin."
- "I could inflate my lifestyle, but I'd rather increase flexibility."

- "I could impress someone briefly, but I'd rather sleep well."

MARGIN CREATES LEVERAGE

Living below your means is when your expenses are consistently lower than your income. That gap is where lots of good things happen. That margin can fund your investments, build your emergency cushion, reduce anxiety, and increase your options.

Without margin, every surprise is a threat. With margin, surprises are manageable.

As pointed out in the book's introduction, the "Wealthy Barber" principle—live below your means, save a fixed percentage, invest consistently, and let compounding do its thing—works because it builds margin.

You don't need to outsmart the market. You need to outlast your impulses.

Defining *enough* helps you do that. Once you know what you're building toward, you're less tempted to chase everything. Then, spending becomes calmer.

Here's a bonus that doesn't get emphasized enough: Living below your means does more than reduce pressure today; it also lowers your financial overhead, so you can invest the difference consistently. As a result, someday work can become optional.

Not because you chased extreme returns. Not because you hit a lottery investment. But because you created a gap between what you earn and what you need. And you let that gap compound for years.

When your lifestyle costs less than your earning power, you create margin. The earlier you build margin, the more years compounding has to work. The more years that compounding works, the less heroic saving you need later.

This is how someone earning a normal income can build extraordinary flexibility. Not overnight. Not dramatically. Just consistently.

SECTION 3: BUILD A FRICTION-FREE SPENDING SYSTEM

DESIGN PREVENTS DRIFT

Now we get practical. If you don't design your spending system, it will design itself. And that usually leads you off course.

A friction-free spending system has three traits:

1. It protects your priorities automatically.
2. It limits impulse damage.
3. It requires minimal daily willpower.

We're not designing budget restrictions here. We're building guardrails.

Restrictions feel like punishment. Guardrails feel like structure. Guardrails don't hinder movement. They prevent disasters.

A restrictive mindset says, "I can't spend on anything." A guardrail mindset says, "I've already handled the important things. The rest is flexible."

The order matters. If you "pay yourself first" (meaning savings and investing happen automatically, before it hits your wallet), then spending becomes simpler. You don't need to run a cost-benefit analysis on every coffee purchase because the system already protects your future. That's freedom.

(We'll dive deeper into the "Pay Yourself First" principle in Chapter 4.)

BUILD IT ONCE. LET IT RUN.

Living below your means doesn't mean squeezing every ounce of joy out of life. You simply create space in your bank account, mind, and future.

Here's a simple way to set this up.

Step 1: Pay Yourself First (Automatically). Set up automatic transfers to savings and investments right after you get paid.

Step 2: Know Your Fixed Costs. Get a rough, honest number. Close enough is close enough. (Remember, we already did this work in Chapter 2.)

Step 3: Create a Guilt-Free Spending Zone. After savings and fixed costs are covered, what's left is yours to spend—no tracking required. You can even create a separate guilt-free spending account.

Step 4: Check in Once a Month. Not obsessively. Just a quick reset.

That's the simple spending system. It doesn't require obsessive daily tracking, constant recalculation, or emotional negotiation every time you swipe. You build the structure once. Then you let it run.

Aligning spending with values is the final piece. This is where intention becomes visible.

If family time matters, you might spend more on experiences and less on status purchases like cars or boats. If flexibility matters, you might prioritize savings over home upgrades. If travel matters, you might drive a paid-off car and fly comfortably to one of your bucket-list destinations.

ALIGNMENT CHANGES PERSPECTIVE

Alignment doesn't reduce spending. It makes it more intentional. You can spend generously on what matters. You just stop spending casually on what doesn't.

And when your spending matches what you value, something interesting happens: You feel less guilty, avoid impulse buys, and grow more confident.

You're no longer wondering if you "should" have bought something. You know why you did or why you didn't.

That certainty is calming. Over time, your spending patterns reflect your priorities and help strengthen your identity. You stop seeing yourself as "trying to be better with money." You start seeing yourself as someone who uses money intentionally.

QUIET MONEY IS POWERFUL

The Moderately Motivated Man doesn't need extreme frugality. He needs clarity. He needs enough. That means building guardrails. That means growing margin.

When those are in place, spending stops feeling like a leak. It starts feeling like a tool.

When money becomes a tool instead of a temptation, it grows quieter. It doesn't demand constant attention. It funds your life without hijacking it.

That's what spending with intention really means. Not less joy. Just more alignment. More clarity.

That brings us back to where we started: Money feels

heavy when it's vague. When your spending becomes intentional, uncertainty disappears. So does much of the weight.

That's not dramatic. It's steady. And steady wins this race.

KEY TAKEAWAYS FROM CHAPTER 3

1. *Why Most Spending Is Reactive.* Most day-to-day spending is driven by lifestyle creep, comparison, convenience, and emotion—not by intention. When seemingly harmless upgrades raise your baseline spending, margin disappears and stress returns.
2. *Define Enough.* If you never define *enough*, you will chase more indefinitely. Separating *rich* from *wealthy* clarifies your priorities and helps you build margin instead of status.
3. *Build a Friction-Free Spending System.* Guardrails, automation, and value alignment protect your priorities without daily willpower. When spending aligns with what matters, money feels lighter and more manageable.

ACKNOWLEDGMENTS

This chapter draws on enduring ideas in behavioral finance and long-term wealth building: that lifestyle creep quietly erodes margin, that comparison distorts priorities, and that defining *enough* is essential to lasting financial peace. The distinction between being rich and being wealthy was memorably articulated by Morgan Housel in *The Psychology of Money*, while the live-below-your-means-and-invest-consistently philosophy echoes the straightforward discipline championed in books like David Chilton's *The Wealthy Barber*.

MODERATELY PAINLESS EXERCISE

DEFINE YOUR "GOOD LIFE"

This is not about cutting everything. It's about clarity. You'll need 10–15 minutes.

Step 1: Identify Your "Good Life" Baseline

On a piece of paper (or in your Notes app), complete this sentence: "A good life for me—not extravagant, not deprived—costs roughly $____ per year."

Don't overthink it. Use your current burn rate from Chapter 2 as a starting point if helpful. Adjust up or down based on what feels honest.

This is not a retirement projection. It's a sufficiency estimate.

Step 2: Define What Must Be Included

List five things that must be part of that "good life." Examples: safe and comfortable housing, reliable transportation, helping to pay for your kids' annual travel, gym membership, eating out once a week, supporting family, hobbies, or time flexibility.

These are not status symbols. They're stability anchors.

Step 3: Identify What Isn't Essential

Now, list two things that are nice but not necessary. Not morally wrong. Not shameful. Just... optional.

Maybe it's upgrading your phone every year. Maybe it's dining out three times a week instead of once. Maybe it's subscriptions you barely use.

This step isn't about eliminating them immediately. It's about seeing the difference between core and creep.

When you define what matters to you, comparisons with others lose their power. You stop chasing someone else's lifestyle because you've named your own.

Money stress often comes from a moving target. "Enough" keeps trending upward. This exercise draws a line in the sand. Not permanently, but intentionally.

If you know what a good life costs, you know what you're building toward. And that clarity makes both spending and saving calmer.

You've just reduced lifestyle creep by awareness alone.

CHAPTER 4

BUILD A SIMPLE FINANCIAL PLAN

CHAPTER SUMMARY

In this chapter, you will replace "winging it" financially with a structure that runs quietly in the background. You'll learn how to "pay yourself first" by automating savings and investing before spending begins, build an emergency cushion that reduces anxiety, and protect against obvious risks without overcomplicating your life. You'll also identify and reduce financial drag from high-interest debt and unnecessary complexity. The goal isn't financial acrobatics or perfection. It's rhythm. A simple plan, implemented once and allowed to repeat, creates margin, stability, and forward momentum without daily negotiation.

SECTION 1: PAY YOURSELF FIRST

STRUCTURE BEATS WILLPOWER

You don't need a complicated financial strategy. You need a simple one that runs even when you're tired.

That's the real difference between people who feel steady about money and people who constantly feel behind. It rarely comes down to intelligence or income. It's almost always about structure.

Chapter 3 was about intention: defining "*enough*," creating margin, living below your means, and creating an intentional spending system. Chapter 4 is where that margin becomes a financial plan.

Not a 47-tab financial dashboard plan. A simple plan.

Simple plans are powerful because they don't need daily heroics. They don't ask you to wake up inspired. They don't require willpower late at night when you're tired and slightly irritated and tempted to make a questionable online purchase.

They just run. So, let's build that by starting with a key concept we mentioned in the last chapter: Pay yourself first.

THE SEQUENCE MATTERS

There's a reason why the "pay yourself first" principle shows up in personal finance books written decades apart. It works. The idea is straightforward: before you pay the electric company, before you pay the streaming services, before you upgrade your phone or order takeout, you pay your future self.

You set aside a fixed percentage of your income for savings or investing. Not just if there's anything left over. First.

This idea traces back at least to *The Richest Man in Babylon*, which in 1926 framed it as "a part of all you earn is yours to keep." Decades later, *The Wealthy Barber* popularized a similar rule in modern language: Save 10% automatically and invest it consistently.

The magic isn't in the exact number. The magic is in the rhythm. Ten percent. Fifteen percent. Five percent if you're just starting. The specific percentage matters less than the consistency.

Here's why. When you rely on leftovers, you get leftovers.

If saving is what happens after spending, it rarely happens in a meaningful way. Because spending expands to fill the space available. There is always something else to buy, fix, upgrade, or temporarily justify. At 20% off, those Jet Skis seemed like a good idea at the time.

But when saving happens first, your spending naturally adjusts to what remains. That shift alone can change your trajectory.

This isn't about deprivation. It's about sequence.

Imagine two people earning the same income. One saves whatever remains at the end of the month. The other automatically transfers 10% on payday. After a few years, the difference is clear. One has good intentions and nagging anxiety. The other has a growing cushion and momentum.

The second guy didn't necessarily try harder. He simply built a rule, which removes the exhausting exercise of negotiating with yourself.

AUTOMATE THE RHYTHM

Automation is your ally here. When your paycheck hits your checking account and, within 24 hours, a fixed percentage moves to a savings or investment account, something powerful happens: You stop seeing that money as available.

You don't feel like you're giving something up. It simply never enters the day-to-day spending arena.

That's not trickery. That's design.

This is also where delayed gratification reenters the picture. Delayed gratification has been framed as suffering in the short term for some distant, abstract reward. But that framing makes it feel imposing. In practice, it's far less dramatic.

It's choosing slightly smaller consumption today in exchange for having options later. It's choosing margin over maximum. It's choosing to let compounding do what it does best: reward patience. (Again, we'll better explain compounding in Chapter 5. Promise.)

Compounding is not flashy. It doesn't trend on social media. It doesn't produce adrenaline. It produces stability.

When you consistently invest even modest amounts, year after year, you eventually reach a moment where growth begins to outpace effort. The money starts doing more of the work.

Compounding works best when contributions are steady. That's why the "pay yourself first" principle matters so much. It forces consistency without requiring constant motivation.

IDENTITY FOLLOWS REPETITION

If you're early in your career, this may seem abstract. If you're mid-career and feel like you started late, it may feel urgent. Either way, the principle is the same: Pick a realistic percentage, automate it, and let it run.

Remember what we said earlier: the number matters less than the rhythm. Ten percent is a classic starting point because it's psychologically manageable and financially meaningful. But if you're carrying debt or rebuilding after a setback, you might start lower. If your expenses are modest, and your income has grown, you might push higher.

The key is this: Make it automatic. Make it consistent. Make it non-negotiable. That's how you build forward motion without drama.

Paying yourself first is not just about retirement. It's about identity.

When you consistently save and invest, you begin to see yourself as someone who builds wealth. That subtle shift changes future decisions. You become less reactive and less impulsive. And, you are less likely to stretch into obligations you can't comfortably sustain.

SECTION 2: PREPARE FOR THE INEVITABLE

LIFE IS PREDICTABLY UNPREDICTABLE

Now let's talk about building that margin. That buffer. That breathing room.

You see, life is unpredictable. Cars break, roofs leak, jobs change, health shifts, parents age, and kids need braces. You can't just hope little Johnny's teeth sort themselves out.

If your financial system has no buffer, every surprise feels like a crisis. If your system has margin, surprises feel inconvenient, not catastrophic.

BUILD THE CUSHION GRADUALLY

This is where the emergency cushion comes in. Traditional advice often says to save three to six months of expenses. That's not wrong, but it can feel overwhelming if you're starting from zero.

Instead of obsessing over the perfect number, focus on progression. First goal: one month of core expenses. Then two. Then three. (Remember that burn rate from Chapter 2? Use that as a guide.)

You're not trying to hoard cash. You're trying to buy breathing room that changes your emotional posture.

When you know that a job hiccup or medical bill won't pull the rug out from underneath you, your decision-making improves. You negotiate differently. You tolerate less nonsense at work. You make career moves from strength, not fear.

That's what an emergency buffer really buys: peace of mind.

It's not glamorous. But it reduces anxiety dramatically.

COVER WHAT WOULD TRULY HURT

This is also where risk management comes into play. Risk management is not pessimism. It's realism.

You don't buy homeowners' insurance because you expect your house to burn down. You buy it because the consequences of a fire would be devastating. You don't carry health insurance because you're fragile. You carry it because medical costs can be extreme.

The goal isn't to over-insure; it's to protect against obvious exposures. That means focusing on these:

- Health insurance
- Disability insurance (especially if you depend heavily on your income)

- Life insurance (if others rely on you financially)
- Basic property coverage

It does not mean insuring every appliance and gadget. It means covering what would truly hurt.

Again, this is about creating a sense of calm.

When you have an emergency cushion and basic protections in place, you reduce the number of scenarios that can genuinely knock you off course.

That doesn't eliminate uncertainty, of course. It contains it. And that reduces fear.

SECTION 3: REDUCE FINANCIAL DRAG

Not All Debt Is Equal

If paying yourself first builds forward motion, and preparing for the inevitable builds protection, reducing financial drag removes friction.

Drag in a financial system often comes from two places: debt and complexity.

Let's start with debt.

Not all debt is equal. A low-interest mortgage on a reasonably priced home is very different from high-interest consumer debt on depreciating purchases.

But here's the universal truth: Interest works both ways. When you invest, interest compounds for you. When you carry high-interest debt, interest compounds against you. That's drag.

If you're paying 18 percent or more on a credit card balance, no investment strategy is going to outrun that.

Reducing high-interest debt is not just a math decision. It's a psychological one.

When debt balances shrink, mental weight shrinks. You free up future cash flow. You increase margin. You simplify your obligations.

There are different strategies for debt payoff. Some focus on the highest interest first; others focus on the smallest balance first, for psychological wins. The method matters less than the commitment.

Pick a strategy. Execute it steadily. Avoid adding new balances. And reduce the financial drag.

SIMPLIFY THE MOVING PARTS

The second source of drag is complexity. Too many accounts. Too many subscriptions. Too many small recurring obligations that nibble away at your margin. Do you really need the monthly premium plan for advanced hydration insights from your smart water bottle?

Complexity drains attention. If you have to keep track of 14 different payment dates and 22 separate recurring charges, your financial system becomes mentally noisy. And exhausting.

Simplifying doesn't mean minimizing everything to monk-like austerity. It means reducing unnecessary moving parts. Here's how that might look:

- Eliminating old accounts and apps
- Canceling unused subscriptions
- Refinancing high-interest obligations
- Aligning bill due dates

Every layer of simplification reduces cognitive load. And that increases consistency.

Remember, the goal is to make money boring. A simple plan does that.

LET THE PLAN RUN

A simple financial plan ultimately looks like this:

- You earn money.
- A fixed percentage automatically moves to savings/investing.
- Your core bills are predictable.
- You have a buffer for surprises.
- You carry sensible protection.
- You reduce high-interest drag and complexity.
- You can spend what's left without guilt.

And then? You live your life. Not constantly tweaking, worrying, or comparing. You adjust occasionally, when income changes, life stages shift, or goals evolve.

But day to day? It runs.

That's what it means to build a simple financial plan. You replace improvisation with structure. You shift from anxiety to clarity. You design instead of react.

None of this requires over-exertion. You simply make decisions once, implement them cleanly, and allow them to repeat.

Pay yourself first. Prepare for the inevitable. Reduce drag.

Those three pillars create margin, protection, and momentum. And when those are in place, money begins to feel different.

Less heavy. Less dramatic. More steady.

Notice the pattern?

KEY TAKEAWAYS FROM CHAPTER 4

1. *Pay Yourself First.* Saving and investing should happen before spending begins. Automating a fixed percentage creates consistency, builds margin, and removes daily negotiation.
2. *Prepare for the Inevitable.* An emergency cushion and basic risk protection turn surprises into inconveniences instead of crises. Stability improves decision-making and lowers anxiety.
3. *Reduce Financial Drag.* High-interest debt and unnecessary complexity erode momentum. Simplifying your system and removing friction enables your plan to run with ease.

ACKNOWLEDGMENTS

The "pay yourself first" principle traces back to George S. Clason's enduring line that "a part of all you earn is yours to keep," the cornerstone of *The Richest Man in Babylon*. A modern, practical version of that same discipline—saving automatically and consistently—was championed for everyday readers in David Chilton's *The Wealthy Barber*. This chapter continues that long-standing tradition: structure over willpower, automation over emotion, and repetition over heroics.

MODERATELY PAINLESS EXERCISE

THE 1% AUTOMATION UPGRADE

Up to this point, we've been observing. Now we install something. You'll need 10 minutes.

Log in to your payroll portal, retirement account, or bank account. Choose one:

- Increase your 401(k) contribution by 1%.
- Increase your automatic investment transfer by 1% of income.
- Set up a new recurring monthly transfer (even $50 counts).

That's it. Not 10%. Not "max it out." Just 1%.

Small enough that you probably won't feel it. Permanent enough that it will matter.

If you're already contributing comfortably, here's what you can do instead:

- Turn on automatic dividend reinvestment.
- Move one manual monthly transfer to automatic.
- Schedule an automatic transfer the day after payday.

The goal is not extra effort. It's the removal of friction. Willpower is unreliable. Automation is patient.

This change may feel minor. Over time, it won't be.

Make the adjustment. Log out. Your system just improved, and it didn't hurt a bit.

CHAPTER 5
INVEST WITHOUT OBSESSING

CHAPTER SUMMARY

In this chapter, you will learn why simple investing strategies often outperform complicated ones. They may not be attention-grabbing, but they are sustainable. We will explore how broad diversification, low costs, and consistent contributions steadily build long-term momentum. You'll see why trying to time the market usually creates more stress than success and how automation protects you from emotional decision-making. Most importantly, you'll understand how compounding works over time and why patience matters more than cleverness. By the end, investing will feel less intimidating, less dramatic, and far more manageable.

SECTION 1: WHY SIMPLICITY WINS

INVESTING ISN'T A SPORT

If you hang around personal finance long enough, you'll eventually encounter someone who treats investing like a competitive sport.

They talk about beating the market. They reference websites you've never heard of. They mention positions, hedges, entry and exit points, and short-term catalysts.

You just sit there, hoping the conversation somehow finds its way back to fantasy football.

The truth is, when most ordinary investors struggle, it's not about intelligence. It's because they make investing too complicated. They chase, tinker, react, and panic. Or they get bored and try to be clever, which is usually not too clever.

The Moderately Motivated Man does not need a high-drama investment strategy. He needs one that works while he's at work. While he's coaching Little League. While he's taking his spouse out to dinner. While he's sleeping.

Simplicity wins because it reduces decisions. And fewer decisions can mean fewer mistakes.

OWN THE MARKET, DON'T OUTGUESS IT

The index philosophy is built on one humble idea: You don't need to outguess everyone else in the market. You can own the market.

Instead of trying to pick the next breakout stock or perfectly time when to get in and out, you buy a broad slice of the entire market (through low-cost index funds) and let capitalism do its slow, imperfect, long-term thing.

It's not flashy. But it's often effective.

Markets go up. Markets go down. Companies rise. Companies fall. Economies expand. Economies contract.

Over long periods, broad markets have tended to grow.

That doesn't mean every year is good. It doesn't mean every decade is smooth. It means that over time, productive businesses tend to create value.

Simplicity says this: Participate in that growth, without trying to predict it.

THE TIMING TRAP

Market timing, on the other hand, promises control. "If I can just get out before the crash..." "If I can just buy before the rally..."

It sounds reasonable, but there's a catch. To time the market successfully, you have to be right twice. You have to know when to get out. And you have to know when to get back in.

Miss one of those moments, and your long-term returns can suffer dramatically.

Even if you're right twice, you'll be tempted to try again. And again. And again. This leads to overconfidence when things go well and regret when they don't.

Simplicity protects you from your own impulses because investing is less about smarts and more about behavior.

BEHAVIOR BEATS BRILLIANCE

Behavioral pitfalls are everywhere:

- Panic selling during downturns
- FOMO buying during booms
- Checking your portfolio too often
- Letting headlines drive decisions

- Believing you've found "the one stock" that changes everything

Most long-term investing mistakes come from emotional reactions. Simplicity reduces emotional triggers. If you own a broad, diversified index fund and contribute consistently, there are fewer decisions to make.

Fewer decisions mean fewer opportunities to sabotage yourself.

You're not trying to win an investment trophy. You're trying to build freedom. That doesn't require financial genius. It requires staying in the game.

There is a counterintuitive truth about investing. Doing less often produces more. Less trading. Less reacting. Less tinkering. Less chasing. More consistency. More time. More compounding.

Simplicity wins because it aligns with human nature. You don't have to become someone else to succeed. You just have to avoid becoming your own worst financial enemy.

Investing should not dominate your mental bandwidth. It should accumulate wealth in the background. If your investment strategy requires constant attention, it's probably too complicated. And that invites anxiety.

By now, it should be obvious that we are not here to create anxiety. We are here to reduce stress and build confidence. And confidence grows when your strategy is understandable.

If you can explain your investment approach in one or two calm sentences, that's a good sign. If it requires a whiteboard and multiple formulas, you're basically trying to run a hedge fund out of your basement.

SECTION 2: HARNESS THE POWER OF COMPOUNDING

GROWTH ON GROWTH

We've mentioned compounding briefly in some of the earlier chapters. Now it's time to give it more attention.

Compounding doesn't seem dramatic. It's not loud. It doesn't trend. It doesn't make headlines.

But it accumulates.

At first, compounding feels almost underwhelming. You invest a few thousand dollars. It grows a little. You invest more. It grows a little more.

Nothing flashy. Think Crock-Pot, not microwave.

Then something subtle begins to happen. The growth starts coming not just from what you add, but from what has already grown. Your money begins earning on its own earnings. That's when compounding shifts from interesting to powerful.

Benjamin Franklin often wrote about the power of money growing over time. One of his most quoted lines sounds almost too simple to be profound, which is exactly why it works: "*Money makes money. And the money that money makes, makes money.*" (And he knew something about the Benjamins.)

The first dollars you invest start working. Then those dollars produce returns. Then those returns begin producing returns of their own.

You don't see fireworks. You see slow acceleration.

TIME WORKS ITS MAGIC

Time is the real superpower. Not brilliant stock picks. Not inside knowledge. Time.

Starting early helps because time has more runway, but starting late is not fatal. This is important. There are people who didn't begin investing seriously until their 40s or 50s —and still built meaningful wealth by committing to consistency.

Early starts are powerful, and late starts are recoverable. Inaction is the real problem.

The gap between early and late is often exaggerated. What matters most is not when you begin but whether you stay consistent once you do.

A modest investor who contributes regularly to a diversified portfolio for 25 years can outperform a brilliant but inconsistent trader.

CONSISTENCY OUTRUNS TALENT

If your system automatically invests every month, you remove the need for motivation, which is notoriously unreliable.

There will be months when markets are scary. There will be months when markets make you feel like a champion. There will be months when you'd rather spend the money elsewhere.

Automation makes investing less about how you feel and more about what you decided in advance. And decisions made calmly are usually better than decisions made in the moment.

Compounding also changes your relationship with delayed gratification. When you see the math, something clicks. That $1,000 invested today doesn't just sit there. It grows. Then it grows on its growth. Then it grows on that growth.

Over decades, small consistent contributions can snowball into large outcomes. Not because you were aggressive. Because you were steady.

Historically, when you consistently invest even modest amounts, year after year, you eventually reach a point where growth outpaces effort. The money starts doing more of the work.

That's when compounding really flexes. It's slow at first. Then steady. Then impressive.

It's like watching a tree grow. Nothing seems to happen for years. Then one day, you notice shade.

SECTION 3: BUILD A LOW-DRAMA INVESTMENT SYSTEM

THREE SIMPLE QUESTIONS

Let's make this practical. An investment system should answer three questions:

1. What do I own?
2. How much do I own of each?
3. How does it keep running without constant input from me?

Asset allocation is simply how you divide your investments among broad categories, typically stocks and bonds. Very roughly speaking, stocks offer growth potential and bonds offer stability.

You don't need a PhD to grasp this.

When you're younger, you might lean more toward growth. As you get closer to needing the money, you may tilt toward stability. The exact percentages matter less than having a plan. The danger isn't choosing 70% instead of 75%. The danger is reacting emotionally when markets move.

BUILD IT ONCE. LET IT DO ITS JOB.

There's no need for drama. Let's keep the structure super simple:

Step 1: Choose Your Core Funds. Broad market stock index funds, plus a bond fund for stability, are often all you need.

Step 2: Set Your Stock/Bond Allocation. Don't overthink it. A common rule of thumb is to subtract your age from 110 to determine the stock portion. (Thus, a 35-year-old would have a 75/25 stock/bond split.) But the number is less important than simply getting started.

Step 3: Automate Contributions. As discussed, this is where most of the value comes from.

Step 4: Rebalance Occasionally. Once or twice a year. Done.

That's it. No hot tips. No constant research. No daily checking. The fewer moving parts, the better.*

Automation is your ally here. If contributions are automatic, you invest during good months and bad months. When markets drop, you buy at lower prices. When markets rise, you benefit from appreciation.

This is called *dollar-cost averaging*, but you don't need to remember the term. Just remember the rhythm. Volatility can feel scary, but consistency calms emotions.

PREPARE FOR VOLATILITY

Markets can drop sharply. Headlines become dramatic. Experts predict doom.

It's uncomfortable, but volatility is not the same as permanent loss. Temporary declines are normal. Permanent abandonment of your strategy is optional, and usually costly.

A low-drama system assumes volatility. It builds in the expectation that markets will fluctuate. It does not require you to guess when that will happen.

Instead of asking, "Should I get out?" you ask, "Have my long-term goals changed?" If the answer is no, your strategy likely doesn't need to change either. Staying steady during volatility is less about courage and more about preparation.

If you know you have breathing room in your spending, an emergency cushion, a diversified portfolio, and a long time horizon, then market swings feel less threatening.

They feel inconvenient, not catastrophic. That difference is enormous.

The Moderately Motivated Man does not need to love volatility. He just needs to weather it. And that comes from having structure.

In addition to volatility, there's another force to account for in long-term planning: inflation. Prices tend to rise over time. Maybe not dramatically every year, but steadily enough that money sitting idly slowly buys less.

A steady investment strategy can help protect your purchasing power from shrinking.

BORING IS SUSTAINABLE

High fees (like those built into some financial products with high expense ratios) quietly erode returns over time. One percent here. Another percent there. Over decades, those can compound in reverse—against you.

A low-cost index approach keeps more of your returns working for you. Again, not dramatic. Just (historically) effective.

Remember, the goal of investing is not to create adrenaline. It's to create independence. As mentioned, it's okay to be boring. Some would say it's preferred. So, *yawn*, let's review it again. The investing playbook is this:

- You contribute regularly.
- You stay diversified.
- You keep costs low.
- You avoid emotional overreactions.
- You give compounding time to work its magic.

If that sounds rather dull, good. Boring investing is often successful investing because boring is sustainable. And sustainable wins.

The Moderately Motivated Man builds systems, invests consistently, ignores most headlines, revisits his plan occasionally, and stays in the game.

Over time, something subtle happens. His money works harder than he does because he stayed steady. He didn't try to outsmart everyone.

You don't need genius, hustle, or obsession. The edge is clarity, consistency, and calm.

Investing does not have to dominate your life. It should quietly fund it.

And when your system runs in the background—low-drama, diversified, and automated—you stop thinking about beating the market. You focus on living your life. That's the win.

DISCLAIMER

*Remember, those of us here at Moderately Motivated Man headquarters publish books and are not financial advisors. Markets involve risk, and past performance is no guarantee of future results. This book is about building simple, consistent systems to reduce stress around money. It is not personalized financial advice. Consult a professional for your individual situation.

KEY TAKEAWAYS FROM CHAPTER 5

1. *Why Simplicity Wins.* Complex investing strategies often fail because they invite overconfidence, timing mistakes, and emotional reactions. Broad diversification, low costs, and fewer decisions reduce errors and improve long-term outcomes.
2. *Harness the Power of Compounding.* Compounding rewards consistency and time more than brilliance. Small, steady contributions invested over decades can grow dramatically because returns begin earning returns of their own.
3. *Build a Low-Drama Investment System.* A diversified, automated, low-cost plan protects you from emotional decisions and market noise. Boring, repeatable investing keeps your money

working in the background while you focus on living your life.

ACKNOWLEDGMENTS

This chapter stands squarely in the low-cost, broad-index investing tradition popularized for modern readers by J.L. Collins in *The Simple Path to Wealth*. The emphasis on owning the market, minimizing fees, automating contributions, and resisting the urge to tinker reflects a long-standing philosophy: Sustainable behavior, not clever prediction, drives long-term results.

MODERATELY PAINLESS EXERCISE

THE PORTFOLIO SIMPLICITY TEST

If your investing strategy is solid, you should be able to explain it simply. You don't need to impress anyone; just understand it yourself.

Step 1: Try to Explain Your Strategy in Three Sentences

Without looking anything up, answer three questions: What do I own? Why do I own it? How often do I change it?

Keep it simple. Examples:

- "I own broad U.S. and international index funds. I own them because they give me diversified exposure at a low cost. I contribute monthly and don't make changes unless my goals change."

- "I use a target-date retirement fund. It automatically adjusts risk over time. I invest consistently and let it rebalance itself."
- "I own a mix of index funds and a small number of individual stocks. The index funds are my foundation. The individual stocks are a small percentage I'm comfortable holding."
- "Most of my portfolio is in individual stocks I've chosen. I believe in those companies in the long term, and I review them periodically. I understand this approach requires more attention and carries more concentration risk."

Now read what you wrote. Does it feel clear? Or does it feel like you're trying to decode your own system?

Step 2: The One-Minute Test

Imagine explaining your three sentences to your spouse, a close friend, or your future self during a market downturn. Could you say it confidently in under a minute?

If yes, your portfolio is probably simple enough. If not, you may be carrying unnecessary complexity.

Write your three sentences somewhere you can revisit them, such as in your Notes app or on a small card tucked into a desk drawer. You're not changing anything today. You're clarifying the rule you intend to follow, and clear rules create calm.

INTERMISSION

A SMALL FINANCIAL EXHALE

If you're reading this, you've made it through the first half of a book about money. That alone deserves a nod.

And think about what you've already accomplished:

- You've faced the numbers.
- You've looked at your spending.
- You've thought about margin.
- You've built a simple financial plan.
- You've embraced low-drama investing.
- You've learned about compounding without dozing off.

That's real progress. Congrats. You've earned a break.

This is not a checkpoint. There are no worksheets here. No financial quiz. No "calculate this right now."

Just a pause. Welcome to the *Calm Corner.*

Imagine a quiet room where nothing is due. No bills are waiting. No markets are flashing red. No one is asking about your five-year projections.

The lights are soft. The chair is comfortable. Your phone is face down.

Your accounts? They're fine. They can wait.

This is the part where you realize that money is already starting to feel lighter. Not because you're any wealthier than before you started this book. Not because everything is solved.

But because you're clearer. And clarity is calming.

You now understand that margin matters, consistency beats brilliance, compounding rewards patience ... and panic is unnecessary.

That's impressive.

So, take ten seconds. Notice your breathing. Notice that nothing is on fire.

You are allowed to learn about money without being in crisis. You are allowed to improve your financial life without urgency. You are allowed to move steadily.

This intermission is proof of that.

When you turn the page, we'll talk about how to thoughtfully grow what you have and protect what you've built.

But not yet. For now, just sit.

Financial peace doesn't arrive with fireworks. It arrives like this. Quiet, uncomplicated, and unhurried.

Whenever you're ready—not because you "should" but because you want to continue building something solid—turn the page.

And if someone asks what you're doing, you can tell them: "I'm investing in my future. Calmly."

CHAPTER 6
INCREASE WHAT YOU EARN

CHAPTER SUMMARY

In this chapter, you'll start seeing your income differently: not just as a paycheck but as one of your most powerful financial assets. We'll talk about how growing your earning ability can multiply everything else you're building, from investments to flexibility. You'll explore why negotiation is clarification, not confrontation, and how small skill upgrades compound over time. We'll also look at how to expand your income without burning out and how to direct raises intentionally instead of letting lifestyle creep absorb them. Growing income isn't about unnecessary hustle. It's about making a few smart moves that increase what your time is worth.

SECTION 1: YOUR INCOME IS AN ASSET

EARNING POWER COMPOUNDS

When most people think about assets, they think about things with price tags. Stocks. Real estate. Retirement accounts. Maybe a business. Something you can log into to check the current value.

But there's an asset that can outperform almost all of those for the first half of your life: your income. More specifically, your ability to earn.

For a Moderately Motivated Man, income can feel like something that simply happens. You go to work. You do your job. You get paid. Rinse and repeat.

But your earning power isn't fixed. It's not static. It's not random. It's a living asset. And like any asset, it can grow.

In fact, for most men in their 20s, 30s, and 40s, earning power is the largest financial lever available. Investments matter. Saving matters. But increasing the amount flowing into the system multiplies everything else.

We talked earlier about compounding in the context of investing. Money earning money. Returns earning returns.

Your skills compound, too. Every skill you develop makes the next skill easier to acquire. Every project you complete builds confidence for the next one. Every uncomfortable conversation (like negotiating pay) makes the next one less intimidating.

Skill compounding can quietly lead to loud results. If you improve your earning capacity by even a small percentage each year—through skill upgrades, better positioning, or smarter career moves—the long-term impact can rival investment returns.

SMALL GROWTH MULTIPLIES

Imagine two men who both invest responsibly. One

keeps his income flat for 20 years. The second steadily increases his income by 3–5% annually, above inflation.

The second man doesn't just get to invest more. He also has more flexibility. He absorbs setbacks more easily. He recovers faster from surprises. He builds margin more quickly.

Income growth amplifies everything else.

A raise doesn't just increase lifestyle potential. It increases investment potential. It accelerates debt payoff. It strengthens your emergency buffer. It shortens the timeline to financial independence.

This is not about chasing titles or becoming a ladder-climbing machine. It's about recognizing that your earning ability is a core financial lever.

NEGOTIATION IS CLARIFICATION

Negotiation is part of that lever. A lot of men avoid negotiating salary, not because they don't deserve more, but because they dislike friction.

They don't want to seem greedy. They don't want to rock the boat. They don't want to risk an awkward moment. They don't want to upset the one part of their life that isn't currently causing heartburn.

But here's the calm truth: Negotiating isn't confrontation. It's clarification. You're not demanding. You're discussing value.

If you've increased your skills, improved your results, taken on more responsibility, or delivered measurable outcomes, a conversation about compensation is not aggressive. It's rational.

It's simply aligning pay with contribution.

Even small increases compound dramatically over

decades. A $5,000 raise early in your career doesn't just add $5,000 once. It increases your future raises. It increases your percentage-based bonuses. It increases your investment contributions. It increases your retirement matches. It increases your breathing room.

Over 20 or 30 years, that one conversation can quietly alter your financial trajectory.

And here's something important for the MMM mindset: Negotiation does not require theatrics; it requires preparation.

Know your numbers. Know your contributions. Know market ranges. Have the conversation calmly.

INCOME CREATES OPTIONALITY

Optionality, the ability to choose rather than react, is an underlying goal of this book. Here's what optionality means:

- I can walk away if I need to.
- I can take a sabbatical.
- I can change roles.
- I can weather a downturn.

Income growth fuels optionality. When income rises, and lifestyle stays reasonable, your margin expands. And that buffer offers freedom.

This is not about hustle for hustle's sake. This is about thoughtful expansion.

You don't need five side businesses. You don't need a personal brand. You don't need to turn every hobby into a monetized channel. You simply need to treat your earning ability as an asset worth tending to.

That might mean earning one strategic certification. Learning one complementary skill that increases your range. Becoming the calm, reliable problem-solver in your organization. Saying yes to one stretch assignment per year. Asking one thoughtful question in a performance review about growth paths.

Small skill upgrades compound like money. And unlike stocks, you have direct control over this asset. You can choose to reinvest in yourself. You can choose to increase your leverage. You can choose to become slightly more valuable each year.

And when earning power rises steadily, everything else in your financial life becomes easier.

Investing becomes less stressful. Saving becomes less tight. Setbacks become less threatening. Long-term goals become more realistic.

You get the idea.

Income is not just a paycheck. It's a platform. And when you treat it like an asset—growing it calmly, deliberately, and sustainably—you create a financial life that feels lighter, not heavier.

SECTION 2: EXPAND WITHOUT BURNING OUT

HUSTLE HAS A COST

There's a version of income growth advice that feels like punishment.

Wake up at 5 a.m. Launch a side hustle. Grind weekends. Outwork everyone. Sleep later. Survive on Red Bull and mid-day hallucinations.

That approach works for some people. It also burns out many more.

Hustle culture rarely admits that burnout is expensive. It costs health. It costs relationships. And sometimes it costs the very income you were trying to increase.

We are not building a frantic money life. We are building a calm one.

CHOOSE SUSTAINABLE EXPANSION

So let's talk about expansion without exhaustion.

Side income can absolutely be powerful. It can accelerate savings, reduce risk, and give you more options. An extra $500 or $1,000 per month directed toward investing or debt reduction can dramatically change timelines.

But it must be thoughtful. Before adding income streams, ask yourself three questions:

- Does this align with my energy?
- Does this build a skill that compounds?
- Does this reduce long-term pressure or increase it?

That third question is the most important. If your side income drains you so much that you spend more to cope—ordering more takeout, buying more "treat yourself" items, or taking stress vacations you can't afford—you've defeated the purpose.

If it compromises your health, sleep, or relationships, the math doesn't work.

SMALL STREAMS COMPOUND

Strategic growth means choosing expansions that strengthen you rather than deplete you. For some men, that might mean consulting occasionally in their existing field. Teaching what they already know. Freelancing a skill they use daily at work. Building a small digital product once and letting it sell quietly. Creating a modest service business that fits naturally into their life.

You do not need explosive growth. Stable growth can compound nicely.

There's something deeply underrated about steady, boring income streams that don't require constant reinvention. They don't look impressive on social media. They don't produce dramatic headlines. But they can build real financial muscle over time.

And often, the best move is not adding a second income stream at all. As we pointed out at the beginning of this chapter, it's about improving the income stream you already have.

BEWARE THE HUSTLE TRAP

Hustle culture equates busyness with progress. More hours equal more ambition. More exhaustion signals more commitment. More chaos indicates more grind.

But busyness is not the same thing as progress. More hours do not automatically equal more wealth. Smarter positioning often beats longer days.

Sometimes the smart move is saying no to something that would pay you now but would distract you from something that compounds over the long term. Sometimes the better move is protecting your evenings, so you can think clearly—and make one smart career move per year instead of five frantic ones.

The Moderately Motivated Man expands when it makes sense. Not because the internet told him he's falling behind. He does not build a second job out of insecurity. He builds additional income out of strategy.

And he remembers that burnout destroys optionality. A burned-out man with a higher salary is not freer. A balanced man with a steadily growing income is.

Expansion should feel like widening a path, not sprinting uphill. It should feel like adding capacity, not adding chaos.

If income growth increases anxiety more than it increases stability, it's misaligned.

The goal is not maximum income at all costs. The goal is sufficient income with growing margin because margin gives you choices.

And choices, not hustle, are what we're really after.

SECTION 3: DIRECT SURPLUS INTENTIONALLY

RAISES ARE INFLECTION POINTS

Let's assume something good happens. You negotiate a raise. You land a better-paying role. Your side project starts generating real income.

Now what?

Here's where many men unknowingly sabotage themselves.

Lifestyle creep shows up quietly. The nicer apartment. The upgraded car. The $20 delivery fee for an $8 burrito. The subtle upgrades everywhere.

None of those is wrong. But if every raise is absorbed

immediately by new spending, margin stays flat. So does freedom.

The key is the intentional direction of that newly earned money. When income rises, decide in advance where the increase goes. Not all of it. But a meaningful portion.

INVEST THE INCREASE

This is where the "invest the raise" philosophy becomes powerful. Imagine you earn $10,000 more this year.

- $5,000 can modestly improve your lifestyle.
- $5,000 can permanently increase your investments.

You feel progress now, and you accelerate freedom later.

Raises are inflection points. They are moments when your financial trajectory can shift upward dramatically.

If each income increase permanently increases your investment rhythm, compounding accelerates. Remember from earlier: *Money makes money. And the money that money makes, makes money.*

Income growth is fuel. Investment is ignition. Together, they create acceleration.

Future-proofing your life doesn't require massive jumps. It requires incremental surplus directed wisely. If you increase your savings or investment rate every time your income grows, retirement doesn't have to be a moving target. It becomes a clear path.

PLAYING THE LONG GAME

This is where the long-game approach begins to make sense. No lottery tickets. No windfalls. Just margin. Consistent investing. Controlled lifestyle growth. Income that gradually rises. Compounding that accelerates over time.

Living below your means in your 30s isn't just about less stress today. It's about creating the possibility of walking away earlier than expected.

Earlier retirement is about more than quitting work. It's about choice. To pivot. To slow down. To work because you want to, not because you have to.

Directing surplus intentionally helps build that choice. The Moderately Motivated Man does not chase income to impress anyone. He increases income to create options.

KEY TAKEAWAYS FROM CHAPTER 6

1. *Your Income Is an Asset.* Your earning ability is one of your most powerful financial levers. Small, steady skill upgrades compound over time, and thoughtful negotiation helps you capture more of that value.
2. *Expand Without Burning Out.* Income growth should make you more stable, not more anxious. Sustainable expansion, whether through skill development or modest side income, builds leverage without sacrificing your health or relationships.
3. *Direct Surplus Intentionally.* Raises and new income are inflection points. When you invest a portion of each increase instead of inflating your lifestyle, margin grows, and compounding accelerates.

ACKNOWLEDGMENTS

This chapter reflects a long-standing behavioral truth in personal finance: Income growth creates leverage only when it is directed intentionally. The emphasis on negotiation, skill development, and assigning raises toward long-term goals aligns with the broader behavior-first tradition in popular personal finance writing—including books such as Dave Ramsey's *The Total Money Makeover*, which emphasize structure and deliberate allocation over financial complexity. Here, those principles are applied through a calmer lens, focused on sustainability and optionality rather than intensity.

MODERATELY PAINLESS EXERCISE

The 15-Minute Market Value Upgrade

Money grows faster when you grow, too. Not through grinding. Through leverage.

Step 1: Pick One Skill That Increases Your Value

Choose one area where a small improvement could increase your earning power. Not ten. One.

If you're unsure, consider one of these buckets:

- *Communication:* writing clearer emails, speaking up in meetings, presentation skills, and negotiation
- *Professional Skills:* mastering one key software tool, improving data literacy, learning

automation shortcuts, and updating a certification
- *Leadership*: delegating better, giving clearer feedback, running tighter meetings, and managing conflict calmly
- *Revenue:* improving client retention, increasing close rates, upselling responsibly, and shortening sales cycles

Pick the one that would most obviously increase your value in your current environment.

Step 2: Take One 15-Minute Action

Now do one small thing to move in that direction: Watch one focused tutorial, read one article, outline one improvement idea, schedule one conversation, or practice one skill deliberately.

Do not enroll in a program. Don't redesign your career. Just 15 minutes. Set a timer. Start. Stop when it rings.

You are not transforming your life today. You are nudging your earning power upward. Small upward nudges compound, too.

Step 3: Schedule the Next Nudge

Before you close your laptop, schedule one more 15-minute block next week.

That's it. Not a commitment to mastery. Just a second rep.

Consistency beats intensity. Two 15-minute sessions are infinitely more powerful than one ambitious plan you never start.

CHAPTER 7
PROTECT WHAT YOU BUILD

CHAPTER SUMMARY

In this chapter, you'll learn how to protect what you've built without turning into a nervous market-watcher. We'll separate volatility from real danger and talk about why downturns are uncomfortable, but normal. You'll see how diversification, reasonable expenses, and margin for error make market swings far less threatening. We'll also tackle the real risk to long-term wealth: your behavior. By setting simple rules and staying aligned at home, you'll make fewer emotional moves and more steady ones.

SECTION 1: UNDERSTAND RISK WITHOUT FEAR

VOLATILITY IS NOT DANGER

If investing were a movie, most people would imagine it as an action film. Charts flashing. Markets swinging. Experts yelling. Headlines screaming words like *plunge, soar, panic, meltdown, record high*, and *historic crash*. It's basically *Die Hard* meets *Wall Street*.

It's a lot. And if you're not careful, you can start to believe that investing is supposed to feel intense. But it's not.

Market volatility is normal. Economic cycles are normal. Recessions are normal. Expansions are normal. Bubbles are normal. Corrections are normal.

None of those situations is a sign that something is broken. They are signs that you are participating in a living system.

The mistake most people make is confusing volatility with danger. Volatility is movement. Danger is permanent loss. Those are not the same thing.

A diversified portfolio going down 15 percent during a rough year is volatility. It feels uncomfortable, but it's movement inside a system that has historically recovered.

Selling everything during that downturn and locking in the loss because you "can't take it anymore"—that's where danger creeps in.

The Moderately Motivated Man doesn't eliminate risk. He understands it, which makes it far less frightening.

MARKETS HAVE SEASONS

Think of it like the weather. If you live somewhere that has seasons, you don't panic every time the temperature drops. You don't assume winter means the end of agriculture. You know it's part of the cycle.

Markets have seasons, too. Bull markets feel like summer. Everything grows. Optimism is everywhere. You start to feel like you're smarter than you really are. You start offering unsolicited investing advice at PTA meetings.

Bear markets feel like winter. Headlines darken. Confidence shrinks. You start to question whether this time is different.

It usually isn't.

Economic cycles are older than the stock market itself. Businesses expand. Credit flows. Overconfidence builds. Something contracts. Then recovery begins. Repeat.

Trying to predict these cycles with precision is a full-time job, and even professionals get it wrong regularly.

Your job is not to predict the cycle. Your job is to survive it.

EXPECT TURBULENCE

This is where the idea of a margin of safety becomes powerful. That simply means you build in room for error. You don't invest money that you'll need next month. You don't build a life that depends on perfect market performance. You don't structure your plan so tightly that one bad year knocks everything over.

You assume volatility will happen because it will. When you expect it, you don't fear it.

This mindset alone separates calm investors from reactive ones. If you believe markets should go up smoothly forever, every downturn feels like betrayal. If you understand markets move in waves, downturns feel like turbulence: uncomfortable but survivable.

REDUCE FRAGILITY

Risk isn't only about markets. It's about job stability.

Health. Unexpected expenses. Family responsibilities. Business cycles.

Protection is holistic. When your financial life has a cushion—savings, diversified investments, and manageable expenses—risk loses its power to scare you into bad decisions.

It's impossible to eliminate uncertainty. You're simply trying to reduce how fragile you are when it shows up, so you don't make mistakes out of fear. Because staying patient is how wealth compounds.

SECTION 2: DESIGN FOR STABILITY

DIVERSIFICATION IS SHOCK ABSORPTION

If Chapter 5 was about building your investment engine, this chapter is about adding shock absorbers.

A vehicle without shock absorbers makes for a bumpy ride. Diversification is the first stabilizer.

You've heard the word before, and it can sound technical. It isn't. Diversification simply means you don't bet your future on one thing.

Not one stock. Not one sector. Not one company. Not one country. Not one asset.

When you own a broad index fund, for example, you are already diversified across hundreds (sometimes thousands) of companies. That alone dramatically reduces the risk that one bad decision wipes you out.

Diversification doesn't eliminate downturns. It reduces the chance of catastrophe. It trades explosive upside for durable growth.

And durable growth is exactly what the Moderately

Motivated Man is after. You are not trying to win a trophy for the highest return in a single year. You are trying to build a system that works across decades.

ZOOM OUT

Long-term thinking naturally stabilizes your decisions. When you measure performance over months, everything feels dramatic. When you measure over decades, drama shrinks.

Zooming out is underrated. If you look at a 30-year chart of the market, the crashes that felt terrifying at the time often look like dips in a long upward slope.

That perspective doesn't make downturns painless, but it adds context.

Designing for stability also means building room for error into your plan. Here's what you can do to make room for error:

- Save slightly more than the bare minimum.
- Avoid high levels of debt.
- Keep your fixed expenses reasonable.
- Maintain an emergency buffer.
- Don't chase speculative trends.

Room for error is a psychological gift to your future self. It says, "You don't have to be perfect."

Perfection-based plans are brittle. They assume you will ride through smooth markets, earn uninterrupted income, and never hit bumps in the road. Flexible plans assume life will get messy—which it always does.

The more rigid your finances are, the more vulnerable you feel. If your mortgage stretches you thin, a job change becomes terrifying. If your car payment eats a large percentage of your income, every repair feels catastrophic. (Suddenly, those annoying extended warranty calls don't sound so crazy.)

If your expenses rise with every raise, progress feels invisible.

MANAGE FIXED COSTS

Stability often comes down to one simple principle: Keep your fixed obligations manageable.

When your overhead is reasonable, volatility becomes inconvenient instead of devastating.

This is also where the "Big Three" anchors begin to matter: housing, cars, and kids. Financial stress is often tied to these three categories.

Housing sets your baseline overhead. Cars can quickly drain your cash flow. Kids amplify both joy and expenses—often at the same time.

A moderate rule of thumb is this: None of these categories should dominate your financial life to the point that everything else feels fragile. A house should provide shelter and comfort, not anxiety. A car should move you, not define you. Kids should inspire planning, not panic.

You don't need exact percentages here. You need awareness. If one of these anchors feels heavy, that's a design issue, not a character flaw. And design can be adjusted over time.

Stability is not flashy. It is deeply underrated. Stability is what enables you to stay invested during downturns, remain calm during recessions, and avoid making decisions you regret five years later.

You cannot control markets. You can control how you

respond. Your behavior is often more dangerous than volatility.

SECTION 3: AVOID SELF-SABOTAGE

BEHAVIOR IS THE REAL RISK

Here's an uncomfortable truth: Markets don't destroy most portfolios; behavior does.

Emotional investing is the quiet killer of long-term returns. It shows up in predictable ways: Buying when headlines are euphoric. Selling when headlines are terrifying. Chasing the "next big thing." Abandoning a strategy because it feels boring.

Comparison makes this worse. Someone at work mentions a stock that doubled. A neighbor talks about a real estate win. A podcast host explains how he "saw it coming."

Suddenly, your steady, diversified plan feels dull.

But dull is usually a good thing. Dull is stable. Dull compounds. Dull works.

SPECULATION NEEDS BOUNDARIES

That said, dull isn't "fun." Or exciting. So there's a reality worth mentioning: If you feel the urge to experiment with a hot tip, a new technology, or something speculative, you don't have to pretend that impulse doesn't exist. Just separate it from your real plan.

If you want to take a swing, keep it small. Think hobby-sized, not future-sized. One percent of your portfolio is entertainment. Fifty percent is like going to Vegas and putting your entire paycheck on black—after a few too many free drinks.

Speculation can be interesting. It can occasionally be successful. But your long-term wealth should never depend on being right about something trendy.

Your strategy builds wealth. Your experiments should never threaten it.

The Moderately Motivated Man does not need to win the short-term comparison game. He needs to win the long-term stability game. And that requires behavioral consistency.

WRITE RULES IN CALM TIMES

Behavioral consistency is not about being unemotional. It's about creating structure that reduces emotional decision-making.

Automation helps. Limited tinkering helps. Written rules help.

You can create a simple strategy for yourself:

- I invest automatically every month.
- I rebalance once per year.
- I do not make changes based on headlines.
- I review my plan annually, not weekly.

Having a written rule turns chaos into protocol. When volatility hits, you don't ask, "What do I feel like doing?" You ask, "What did I decide in advance?"

Decisions made in calm conditions are usually better than decisions made in fear.

PROTECT ALIGNMENT AT HOME

This is also where relationship stability comes into play. Money tension within a partnership often rises during volatility. If markets drop and one partner is anxious while the other is calm, friction can appear.

Regular financial communication with your spouse or significant other matters. You don't need all-day summits or spreadsheet presentations. You need shared understanding.

A simple quarterly check-in works wonders:

- Where are we?
- Are we still aligned?
- Are we comfortable with our plan?
- Do we need to adjust our spending?

When both partners understand the long-term nature of investing, downturns feel less threatening. Clarity reduces conflict. And who enjoys tension in the household?

DON'T OVER-DO IT

Another subtle form of self-sabotage is over-monitoring. Checking your investments daily is like weighing yourself after every meal. You'll see fluctuation, but you won't see progress because progress shows up over years.

Frequent checking amplifies emotion, which can lead to unnecessary (or even harmful) action. Protecting what you build is largely about protecting yourself from yourself. Markets are noisy. The media is dramatic. We humans are reactive.

Your edge is having a smart, simple plan—and staying the course when others wobble.

This doesn't mean you ignore reality. It means you filter

it. When markets drop, ask: Has the long-term thesis changed? Or is this a normal cycle?

When someone brags about short-term gains, ask yourself, "Is that replicable? Or is that luck with puffed-up storytelling?"

When you feel the urge to act, ask yourself, "Is this strategic? Or is it emotional?"

The Moderately Motivated Man is not immune to fear. He is prepared for it, which makes it manageable.

If you have a diversified portfolio, reasonable expenses, an emergency buffer, a long-term mindset, automated investing, and shared understanding at home, then volatility becomes part of the plan, not a threat to it.

Protection is not about armor. It's about resilience that says, "This might get uncomfortable, but I'll still be standing."

Because when downturns pass, and they do, those who remained standing participate in the recovery. Compounding resumes. Confidence deepens. Optionality grows.

Protecting what you build is less about dramatic moves and more about steady posture. You don't flinch at every headline. You don't chase every trend. You don't panic at every dip.

You breathe. You review your structure. You stay consistent and invested. That's how wealth can compound across decades.

KEY TAKEAWAYS FROM CHAPTER 7

1. *Understand Risk Without Fear.* Volatility is normal movement, not permanent danger.

   When you expect downturns and build margin for error, market swings feel uncomfortable but survivable.

2. *Design for Stability.* Diversification, reasonable expenses, and room for error make your finances less fragile. A stable financial structure enables you to stay invested through cycles without panic.
3. *Avoid Self-Sabotage.* Emotional decision-making is a major threat to long-term wealth. Written rules, automation, limited monitoring, and shared alignment at home protect your strategy from impulsive moves.

ACKNOWLEDGMENTS

This chapter builds on the long-term discipline championed by John C. Bogle, who consistently argued that investor behavior, not market volatility, is the greatest threat to long-term results. The emphasis on diversification, staying the course, and designing systems that reduce emotional decision-making aligns with the enduring philosophy of resilience over prediction.

MODERATELY PAINLESS EXERCISE

Instructions for a 20% Drop

Markets fall. It's not a possibility. It's a pattern. At some point, your portfolio will drop 20%. Maybe more. Yikes. The time to decide how you'll respond is not during the drop. It's now.

Step 1: Write What You Will Not Do

On a sheet of paper (or in your Notes app), complete this sentence: "If the market drops 20%, I will not _____."

Examples: Sell everything, check my accounts daily, change my long-term strategy, make decisions based on headlines, or assume this time is different.

Be specific. This is your guardrail.

Step 2: Write What You Will Do

Now complete this sentence: "If the market drops 20%, I will _____."

Examples: Continue investing as planned, rebalance if necessary, review my long-term plan calmly, wait 30 days before making any structural changes, or re-read my investment plan from Chapter 5.

This is your anchor.

Step 3: Write Why

Finally, add one short explanation: "I follow this plan because _____."

Examples: Markets recover over time, volatility is normal, my timeline is long, or panic is more dangerous than downturns.

Keep it simple. This is not a thesis.

When markets fall, emotions rise. This page exists to lower the temperature. Store it somewhere you can easily find it.

You are not predicting the future. You are deciding your behavior in advance because behavior, not volatility, is often the real risk.

CHAPTER 8
PLAN FOR THE LONG TERM

CHAPTER SUMMARY

In this chapter, we zoom out. You'll see how to approach retirement without panic by turning uncertainty into something you can measure. We'll look at how managing the Big Three—housing, cars, and kids— shapes your long-term freedom. You'll explore how to enjoy life now while still building security later, and why retirement is less about hitting a magic number and more about building a system that works. Finally, we'll think about what all of this is really for—stability, flexibility, and eventually, legacy. Long-term planning isn't about predicting everything. It's about building something steady enough to handle change.

SECTION 1: RETIREMENT WITHOUT PANIC

TURN UNCERTAINTY INTO MATH

Retirement is one of the few financial topics that can make a calm, rational adult feel like a teenager who forgot to study for the final exam. And the test is in an hour.

The word alone carries pressure. It sounds like a finish line. A cliff. A countdown clock. A question mark.

"How much do I need?" "What if I run out?" "What if I save too little?" "What if I save too much?"

Most retirement anxiety doesn't come from doing something wrong. It comes from not knowing where we stand. We imagine a giant number—$2 million, $3 million, who knows—floating in the distance like some mystical target. And because the number feels abstract, we either obsess over it or avoid it entirely.

Let's remove the haze. Retirement is math. At its core, retirement planning asks two calm questions: How much does your life cost? For how long does it need to be funded?

That's it. Not, "How rich do I want to look?" or, "How do I beat everyone else?" It's really asking, "What does my life require?"

If your lifestyle costs $80,000 a year and you expect to receive $30,000 from Social Security or a pension, you need to generate $50,000 per year from your investments.

Now we're in manageable territory.

There's a widely discussed guideline called the "4% rule." It suggests that if you withdraw around 4% of your portfolio per year (adjusted for inflation), your money has historically had a strong chance of lasting 30 years or more.

It's not a promise or a guarantee. But it is a starting point.

If you will need $50,000 per year from investments, that means you likely need a portfolio of around $1.25 million. (Because 4% of $1.25 million is $50,000.) That number might feel big. Or small. Or intimidating. Or achievable.

But notice what just happened. The mystical cloud turned into arithmetic, and math is calmer than the great unknown.

The real driver of retirement confidence isn't hitting a perfect number. It's about building flexibility. Markets fluctuate. Expenses change. Life evolves.

The more flexible your lifestyle and the more margin you build, the less pressure on your portfolio.

MANAGE THE BIG THREE EARLY

This is where the Big Three enter the chat: Housing. Cars. Kids. Most long-term financial strain doesn't come from coffee purchases. It comes from these anchors:

- A mortgage that consumes half your income
- Two car payments that feel permanent
- Education expenses that squeeze tighter than expected

If you intentionally manage the Big Three over decades —buying a house that doesn't own you, driving cars that don't require applause, and planning realistically for education—you lower your lifelong overhead.

That lower overhead makes retirement math friendlier. A man who needs $60,000 per year in retirement is in a very different position than one who needs $120,000.

Lifestyle discipline early becomes freedom later. That's not deprivation; that's architecture.

LIVING IN RETIREMENT

Now let's talk longevity, the other silent fear. We're living longer. Retiring at 65 could mean funding 30 years. Retiring at 55 might mean funding 40.

That sounds intimidating, until you remember something important: You are not stockpiling cash in a vault. You are investing in productive assets. Your money continues working.

Retirement is not "live off a pile." It's "live off a system." Your portfolio does the job while you finally get to play golf without worrying about your money.

There will be down years. That's normal. But diversified investments have historically grown over long periods, even while supporting withdrawals.

When people panic about running out of money, they often imagine their bank account shrinking. But a well-built retirement plan is dynamic. Withdraw modestly. Stay diversified. Adjust when necessary. Let time continue to do its work.

Now, let's lightly mention taxes. Most men encounter three primary investment buckets:

- Tax-deferred (401(k)s or traditional IRAs)
- Tax-free (Roth accounts)
- Taxable brokerage accounts

Each has a role. Tax-deferred accounts reduce taxes now but are taxed later. Roth accounts are taxed now but grow tax-free. Taxable accounts offer flexibility.

The goal isn't to master the tax code. It's building flexibility, so you're not forced into one rigid withdrawal strategy later. Retirement confidence comes from options.

INDEPENDENCE OVER ESCAPE

The truth is, you don't need to "retire" dramatically. You want to reach financial independence, the point at which work is optional. And optional work feels very different from mandatory work.

Some men retire and consult lightly. Some pivot to passion projects. Some volunteer. Some rest. Some reinvent.

The goal isn't to escape. It's to achieve autonomy, with the opportunity to say yes or no without fear.

You do not need a flawless forecast. You need a reasonable plan. Manageable overhead. Steady investing. Diversified tax buckets. Sustainable withdrawals.

Retirement without panic isn't about predicting the future. It's about designing a life where the future doesn't frighten you.

SECTION 2: BALANCE NOW VS. LATER

THE TRADE-OFF

There's an unspoken tension in every long-term financial conversation. Save more now, so you can enjoy later. Or, spend now, so you don't resent later.

Both instincts are valid. If you over-index on the future, life can feel like a waiting room. If you over-index on the present, the future can feel daunting.

The Moderately Motivated Man isn't choosing one. He's integrating both.

This is where delayed gratification deserves a second look. You don't need to deny yourself a good life. You can design the order in which it unfolds.

When you intentionally design spending, enjoyment becomes clearer. A weekend trip paid for in cash feels different than one layered onto credit. A dinner enjoyed within margin feels different than one eaten with a side of guilt.

We aren't preaching penny-pinching. We're talking about spending in ways that make life easier and more enjoyable.

SECURE THE BASE FIRST

If you fast-forward 20 years, what would you regret more, spending too much now or never fully enjoying this phase?

The answer depends on your temperament and stage of life. But the strategy stays the same: Build the base first, and then enjoy the excess intentionally.

The base includes a steady savings rhythm, manageable housing costs, and an automatic investment plan. Once that foundation exists, spending becomes creative rather than reactive.

You can upgrade selectively. Travel deliberately. Invest in experiences that matter.

This is where your definition of enough returns. When you define *enough*, you stop chasing everything. And when you stop chasing everything, you can enjoy what you have.

ENJOY THE MARGIN INTENTIONALLY

Income increases don't automatically require lifestyle increases. Sometimes the most powerful moves are invisible. Keep living roughly the same way. Invest the difference. Let compounding supercharge the raise.

That's not boring; it's strategic. The Moderately Motivated Man doesn't postpone joy indefinitely. He avoids tying joy to permanent obligations.

Experiences are flexible. Overhead is sticky. A memorable trip ends. A seven-year car loan lingers—long after the new-car smell is replaced by the aroma of stale French fries.

Balancing now versus later is not about choosing one over the other. It's about creating a rhythm: Secure the base. Enjoy the margin. Repeat.

When both are happening at once, you'll feel less tension.

SECTION 3: THINK BEYOND YOURSELF

MODEL STABILITY

Long-term planning eventually moves beyond spreadsheets. The question shifts from, "Will I be okay?" to, "What does okay mean for the people connected to me?"

Money is about numbers, but it's also about continuity.

If you have children, they're watching more than you think: not your net worth but your habits. They notice whether you panic or plan. Whether purchases are impulsive or intentional. Whether money conversations are tense or calm.

Financial education begins with modeling. You don't need lectures. You can set an example.

When children see money treated as a tool, not a stress trigger, that lesson sticks.

REDUCE STRESS FOR OTHERS

Generational thinking isn't about building a dynasty. It's about reducing chaos for your family. That might mean having basic estate documents in place, updating beneficiaries, and ensuring someone understands where the accounts are located.

It isn't glamorous work, but it's loving work.

There's also a subtler legacy that often matters more than inheritance: stability. When your financial life is steady, you're more patient, more present, and less reactive.

Choosing a house you can comfortably afford protects more than retirement. It protects your mood.

Driving a car that fits your life rather than your ego reduces background pressure.

Planning thoughtfully for kids isn't about funding everything. It's about setting expectations.

Leaving a legacy is more than just leaving money. It's also about helping the next generations understand how to take the stress out of their financial lives.

MONEY AS A FRAMEWORK

At some point, the question becomes, "What is my money for right now?" If retirement is funded and risk is managed, what does your current capital support? Flexibility. Generosity. Creative risk. Presence.

Long-term planning is not about hoarding. It's about aligning money with meaning.

Financial flexibility is powerful, but it requires some thought. Money doesn't define your purpose. It simply creates the space to explore it.

You don't need extreme wealth to think generationally. You need clarity and a plan that runs quietly in the background.

What does success look like? Bills paid. Options available. Pressure reduced. Lessons passed down.

When you plan for the long term, you're not predicting every outcome. You're building a life that can absorb change.

When money becomes a framework—steady, supportive, and invisible—you're free to focus on what actually matters. That's the quiet victory.

MONEY WITH A PURPOSE

Back to the question, "What is this money for now?"

Extra money can be used for a lot of things. It can fund charitable giving, support your kids, help with aging parents, or simply give you more control over your time.

The goal is not to hoard. And it's not to spend just because you can. It's to decide what role money should play once survival is no longer the main event.

For one guy, that may mean funding travel while he's still healthy enough to enjoy it. For another, it may mean helping a child graduate with less debt. For another, it may mean giving more, working less, starting something new, or building a cushion large enough that his family feels steady.

There is no single correct answer, but there should be an answer.

That's where money becomes more than numbers. It becomes a tool for shaping the life around you.

Long-term planning is not just about reaching "enough." It's about deciding what enough allows you to do next.

KEY TAKEAWAYS FROM CHAPTER 8

1. *Retirement Without Panic.* Retirement planning becomes calmer when you replace vague targets with arithmetic. Manage your overhead, build flexibility, and focus on financial independence rather than a dramatic finish line.
2. *Balance Now vs. Later.* Long-term security and present enjoyment are not opposites. Secure your financial base first, then enjoy your margin intentionally without inflating permanent obligations.
3. *Think Beyond Yourself.* Stability, clarity, and preparation create a legacy that extends beyond money. When your financial system runs quietly, you reduce stress for others and create space for purpose.

ACKNOWLEDGMENTS

This chapter references the widely discussed "4% rule," first articulated by financial planner William Bengen in 1994 and later examined in the Trinity Study. These strategies are not guarantees but useful starting points for translating retirement uncertainty into practical arithmetic and building confidence through structure rather than speculation.

MODERATELY PAINLESS EXERCISE

THE 25X PERSPECTIVE

Retirement planning often feels abstract. Let's make it math.

Step 1: Start With Your "Enough" Number

From Chapter 3, what does a steady, good life cost you per year? Write that number: $____ per year.

Now subtract any reliable income you expect to receive in retirement: Social Security (estimated annual benefit per SSA.gov), pension income, and other guaranteed income streams.

What remains is the amount your investments would need to provide annually. Write that number: $____ per year from investments.

Step 2: Multiply by 25

Take that annual investment number and multiply it by 25. Why 25?

Because withdrawing about 4% per year from a diversified portfolio has historically allowed money to last for decades. And 4% is simply 1 ÷ 25.

If you have 25 times your annual spending invested, withdrawing roughly 4% per year equals one year of income.

Example: If you need $40,000 per year from investments, calculate $40,000 × 25 = $1,000,000.

No guarantees. No magic. Just math.

Step 3: See Where You Stand

Now, take a glance at your current invested assets (retirement accounts + brokerage accounts). How far along are you toward that 25x number? You are not judging. You are understanding where you are today.

Closer than expected? Farther than hoped? Somewhere in between?

This isn't a deadline. It's a direction. The goal is perspective. When you translate uncertainty into math, the future feels less mysterious.

Close the calculator. You now have a little more clarity.

CHAPTER 9
STAY THE COURSE

CHAPTER SUMMARY

In this chapter, we'll talk about the part of money management most people underestimate: staying power. You already know the basics. The challenge is not knowledge; it's temperament. We'll explore why boredom, fear, and impatience derail otherwise solid plans, and how consistency beats being clever over time. You'll see how automation builds confidence, why playing your own game protects your peace, and how identity shapes long-term outcomes. Wealth rarely grows in dramatic bursts. It grows through repetition. Staying the course isn't passive. Disciplined patience turns a good plan into lasting freedom.

SECTION 1: WHY MOST PEOPLE QUIT

BOREDOM IS A RISK

By the time someone reaches this point in a money book, they often know the basics.

They understand saving. They understand investing. They understand that living below their means creates margin. They understand that compounding rewards patience.

The problem isn't knowledge. The problem is staying power.

Many financial plans don't fail because they were flawed. They fail because someone got bored, scared, or impatient.

Boredom is underrated as a financial risk. A steady, diversified investment plan is not exciting. It doesn't produce daily drama. It doesn't generate jaw-dropping stories you can tell at dinner parties.

"I automatically invested in a low-cost index fund again this month." No applause. Not even a mild fist bump.

The human brain craves stimulation. It likes novelty and action.

Long-term investing offers very little of that, which is why people tinker. They check accounts too often. They move money around. They chase trends. They abandon steady plans for "better opportunities."

Not because they're reckless. Because they're restless.

FEAR FEELS URGENT

Market fear is the other major culprit. When headlines scream recession... When markets drop 20%... When friends start texting, "Did you see what's happening?"... Even a well-designed plan can feel shaky.

In those moments, logic takes a back seat to emotion. You don't want to be "wrong." You don't want to "lose everything." You don't want to look foolish for staying calm.

So people sell. They retreat. They freeze. And then, often, they miss the recovery.

Impatience rounds out the trio. We live in a culture of speed. Fast shipping. Fast answers. Fast entertainment.

Compounding is slow. You contribute for years before it feels meaningful. You watch modest growth. You wonder if it's working. And because the early years look underwhelming, some people abandon the plan before the acceleration phase begins.

TEMPERAMENT WINS

The irony is that quitting usually happens right before the system starts rewarding patience. This is why staying the course is less about intelligence and more about emotional management.

Financial success is often a test of temperament. Can you stay steady when it's boring or scary, or when others appear to be sprinting ahead?

Staying invested during a downturn feels uncomfortable. Continuing to invest during a downturn feels even more uncomfortable. But historically, those uncomfortable stretches are where long-term returns are seeded.

None of this requires heroic bravery. It requires perspective. Markets have cycles. Economies expand and contract. Asset prices rise and fall. Volatility is not a bug in the system. It is the system.

If you expect smooth upward lines, you'll be disappointed. If you expect turbulence, you'll be prepared. Preparation lowers panic.

There's also a subtle psychological trap that catches

many intelligent people: the belief that they can outthink the market. After all, you've built a career. You solve problems. You make decisions. You've gotten good at figuring things out.

But investing rewards humility and punishes overconfidence.

The market does not care about your résumé. It does not care about your hunch. It does not reward brilliance in the short term. It rewards discipline over the long term.

The Moderately Motivated Man doesn't need to be the smartest investor in the room. He needs to be the most consistent.

Consistency doesn't make headlines, but it often builds freedom.

Quitting feels active. Staying feels passive. But in long-term finance, staying is the action. The more you understand that, the more patient you become.

SECTION 2: CONSISTENCY BUILDS CONFIDENCE

STRUCTURE REPLACES WILLPOWER

Earlier in the book, we explored how clarity leads to confidence. But in practice, consistency is what makes that confidence stick.

When you know where you stand, understand your spending, have built a simple plan, and have automated your investments, you don't have to rely on willpower. You rely on structure.

Structure is what turns good intentions into durable outcomes.

Think about habit stacking (which we cover in depth in *The Moderately Motivated Man's Guide to Habits*). If you've built a habit of brushing your teeth, you can attach flossing to it. The first habit anchors the second.

Finance works the same way. If every paycheck automatically sends money to retirement, emergency reserves, and brokerage investments, then investing becomes attached to income.

You don't decide every month. You don't debate every month. You don't re-evaluate your future every month. You let the system execute the decision you made when you were calm.

Automation is discipline without drama. It removes daily emotion from long-term strategy because emotion is where many plans break.

There will be months when markets look overheated. There will be months when markets look terrifying. There will be months when you feel tempted to move your money toward something more exciting.

Automation protects you from yourself. It turns consistency into default behavior.

IDENTITY DRIVES BEHAVIOR

But there's a deeper shift happening here, one that goes beyond mechanics. At some point, you stop seeing yourself as "a guy trying to get better with money." You begin to see yourself as "a man who handles money calmly."

That identity shift is subtle but transformative. Identity drives behavior more reliably than motivation. If you see yourself as someone who panics during downturns, you will likely panic. If you see yourself as someone who stays steady, you're more likely to do just that.

The Moderately Motivated Man doesn't chase financial heroics. He builds financial habits. He invests regularly. He adjusts thoughtfully. He reviews periodically, not obsessively.

Confidence grows from repetition. Every month that your system runs quietly reinforces the idea that "This works." Every year that passes without drama reinforces the thinking, "I can handle this."

Confidence isn't built from one big win. It's built from small, repeated winning actions.

There's also something important about time here. The longer you stay consistent, the less dramatic the fluctuations feel. A 10% market drop feels catastrophic in year one. In year fifteen, it feels like the weather.

You've seen storms before. You've seen recoveries before. Experience reduces emotional volatility. And that's a powerful compounding effect in itself.

THE COPILOT FACTOR

Let's also address something extremely important: the copilot factor. For many men, money decisions are not solo endeavors. As we discussed in Chapter 7, a domestic partner is often involved.

Staying the course is much harder when one person panics and the other dismisses. Financial consistency works best when it's shared.

That doesn't mean you need weekly State of the Union meetings with spreadsheets projected on the wall. It means having regular, calm conversations. "What's our long-term plan again?" "Are we comfortable with our savings rate?" "If markets drop, are we still aligned?"

If you're out of sync, don't argue about the market or your spending levels. Discuss the margin of safety you both seek. It's easier to have this conversation.

When both partners understand the strategy, volatility becomes less threatening. You're not reacting alone. You're reinforcing each other.

Calm is contagious. So is panic. Choose which one you cultivate.

Staying the course together strengthens not just portfolios but relationships. And that's a big part of the real return.

SECTION 3: PLAY YOUR OWN GAME

COMPARISON IS A TRAP

There's a quiet poison in a world fueled by social media: comparison. (We've discussed this earlier in the book, but it's worth repeating.)

Someone is always making more, investing differently, retiring earlier, buying bigger, or scaling faster. If you measure your financial life against the loudest voices in the room, you will always feel behind.

Which is why playing your own game matters.

Your game is defined by many factors: Your lifestyle. Your values. Your risk tolerance. Your timeline. Your definition of *enough*.

Enough is not a universal number. For one man, enough means modest housing, strong savings, and time flexibility. For another, enough includes travel, philanthropy, and supporting extended family. Both can be valid.

What becomes dangerous is chasing someone else's version. If your buddy upgrades houses every five years and stretches financially to do it, that's his game. If a colleague day-trades aggressively and boasts about returns, that's his game. If an influencer retires at 35 and monetizes every move, that's their game.

The Moderately Motivated Man is not trying to win their game. He's trying to win his.

Here's winning his game: Bills paid. Savings growing. Stress manageable. Margin expanding. A plan in place. That's it.

When you define *enough* clearly, comparison loses power. If you know you need $80,000 per year to live comfortably, and your system supports that trajectory, someone else's $200,000 lifestyle becomes irrelevant.

MEASURE AGAINST YOURSELF

There's also a deeper peace in personal metrics. Instead of asking, "Am I ahead of others?" ask, "Am I improving relative to my past?"

Did your savings rate increase slightly? Did your debt decrease? Did your investments continue uninterrupted? Those are meaningful metrics. They're less glamorous, but they matter.

Playing your own game also means adjusting when life changes. Health shifts. Careers pivot. Family dynamics evolve. Rigid financial ideology rarely survives real life. But a flexible, principle-based system does.

You know the core principles by now (but let's lock them in): Live below your means. Invest consistently. Diversify. Avoid emotional overreaction. Define *enough*.

Within those guardrails, there is room for adaptation.

CHOOSE QUIET OVER DRAMA

Now let's come back to something we've mentioned all book long: Calm.

Staying the course is easier when your life isn't over-leveraged. When housing is manageable. When car payments aren't suffocating. When savings are automatic.

You've built shock absorbers, which make bumps survivable. Without them, every dip feels existential. With them, dips feel uncomfortable but temporary.

This is where behavior becomes destiny. Markets may not be predictable, but you can be.

Over a decade, small patterns shape your identity. The man who checks his accounts ten times a day remains anxious. The man who reviews quarterly remains steady.

Wealth is rarely built in dramatic bursts. It's built in ordinary months that look forgettable at the time, when your most audacious money move that month was splurging on the extra guac.

The people who build durable wealth are often the ones who tolerate the boredom of doing nothing. They don't need constant reassurance that the system is working. They understand that most of the compounding happens quietly, and that silence is a feature, not a bug.

There's also a humility that develops when you play your own game long enough. You stop needing to compare because you've seen enough cycles to know that short-term wins rarely tell the whole story.

Staying the course is not passive; it's disciplined patience. It's choosing repetition over reaction. It's deciding that you don't need a different plan every time the world feels loud.

And one day, without a dramatic turning point, you'll

realize something subtle: your money no longer feels heavy. Because you have a supportive framework.

At that point, money stops dominating your mental space.

That's when the real return appears. Not just a larger portfolio. A quieter mind.

KEY TAKEAWAYS FROM CHAPTER 9

1. *Why Most People Quit.* Financial plans rarely fail from a lack of knowledge. They fail from boredom, fear, or impatience. Staying invested through discomfort is what enables compounding to work.
2. *Confidence → Consistency.* Structure builds confidence, and confidence reinforces consistency. Automation and shared alignment reduce emotional decision-making and protect long-term progress.
3. *Play Your Own Game.* Comparison disrupts clarity. When you define *enough* and measure progress against your own life, wealth grows quietly, and peace builds with it.

ACKNOWLEDGMENTS

This chapter's emphasis on temperament over intelligence reflects the broader field of behavioral finance, shaped by researchers such as Daniel Kahneman and Richard Thaler, whose work proved that our financial mistakes are actually predictable patterns. It also aligns with practitioner voices like Nick Murray, who has long argued that long-term investment success depends far more on disciplined behavior than on market forecasting skill.

MODERATELY PAINLESS EXERCISE

THE 30-DAY RULE

Long-term investing isn't won by intelligence. It's won by restraint.

Step 1: Write Your Cooling-Off Rule

Write your cooling-off rule in your own words. For example: "I do not change my investment strategy without a 30-day waiting period."

That means no reallocating, switching funds, selling based on headlines, or chasing trends.

You can research, think, and take notes. But you do not act for 30 days.

Step 2: Add One Exception

Write one clear exception where a change would be justified. Examples: A major life change (such as retirement, divorce, or inheritance). A shift in long-term goals. Or a documented, written change in risk tolerance.

This keeps the rule rational rather than rigid.

Step 3: Define Who You're Becoming

Now finish this sentence: "I am the kind of investor who _____."

Examples: Thinks in decades, not headlines. Prioritizes consistency over cleverness. Accepts volatility as the price of long-term growth. Values discipline over prediction.

This is not fluff. Behavior follows identity.

When markets swing or headlines shout, you won't rely on willpower. You'll rely on your rule.

CHAPTER 10

LIVE A CALM MONEY LIFE

CHAPTER SUMMARY

In this final chapter, we'll bring everything together. A calm money life isn't about maximizing returns or chasing complexity; it's about building systems that run quietly in the background. We'll explore what financial peace truly feels like, how to avoid "complexity creep," and why simplicity becomes more powerful over time. When income has a plan, spending is aligned, investing is automated, and risk is managed, money stops dominating your thoughts. It becomes a backdrop. The goal was never obsession or perfection. It was lighter living—reducing weight so you can focus on what matters.

SECTION 1: WHEN MONEY STOPS DOMINATING

INTO THE BACKGROUND

There's a subtle moment that doesn't arrive with fireworks, when money shifts from being a daily mental presence to a background system.

You don't wake up thinking about your bank balance. You don't feel a jolt of anxiety before checking your accounts. You don't replay last month's expenses in your head while brushing your teeth. Instead, you're free to ponder important things, like chicken parm or meatball parm for dinner.

Money is still there. It just isn't loud or heavy.

You're not trying to create wealth as spectacle, status, or scorekeeping. Just wealth as a quiet foundation.

Earlier in this book, we explored how clarity reduces anxiety, how confidence builds consistency, and how consistency compounds into freedom. This is where those threads weave together.

When your income has a plan. When your spending aligns with your values. When your savings are automated. When your investments are diversified. When your risk is managed. When your long-term plan is grounded in math, not mythology. That's when money stops asking for attention.

Your systems run quietly. Paychecks arrive. Automatic transfers happen. Bills are paid. Investments ebb and flow—sometimes up, sometimes down—but within a plan you understand.

You don't need daily supervision. You need periodic awareness. There's a difference.

STABILITY CHANGES IDENTITY

You care about your money. You just don't let it dictate

your mood. A volatile market day doesn't ruin your evening. A strong market month doesn't inflate your ego.

You've seen cycles. You expect cycles. You've built for cycles. As a result, your nervous system relaxes.

For many men, money anxiety isn't about greed. It's about vulnerability. "What if I can't provide?" "What if I miscalculated?" "What if I lose what I built?" Those are deeply human fears.

A calm money life doesn't eliminate uncertainty. It reduces exposure to unnecessary fragility. You've lowered overhead. You've built margin. You've diversified risk. You've avoided speculation as a strategy.

So uncertainty now feels manageable. This is where a shift in identity solidifies. You're no longer "trying to get better with money." You're someone who runs a calm financial system.

When money stops dominating, you think about other things more. Health. Relationships. Curiosity. Contribution.

Money becomes what it was always supposed to be: a tool, not a master.

DESIGN ENDURES

And here's the part that matters most for the Moderately Motivated Man: You didn't get here through obsession; you got here through design.

That matters because obsession burns out. Design endures.

An anxious money life requires constant vigilance. A calm money life requires structure and trust in that structure.

Trust grows from repetition. If your system has worked

for five years, you trust it more than in month five. If it has worked through a downturn, you trust it even more.

Confidence compounds, too. Eventually, money moves from the foreground of your thoughts to the background of your life.

And that's not boring. That's freedom.

SECTION 2: WHAT FINANCIAL PEACE FEELS LIKE

PEACE IS NOT EXTRAVAGANCE

Financial peace is often misrepresented. It's portrayed as luxury, excess, or extravagance.

In practice, it feels much simpler. It feels like control over time. Not total control—life never grants that—but increased flexibility.

You don't need to take every opportunity that pays. You don't need to stay in environments that drain you. You don't need to panic over short-term volatility. You can choose more deliberately.

Optionality is the reward. Optionality says, "I don't have to." I don't have to accept the first offer. I don't have to tolerate chronic stress. I don't have to make decisions from fear.

Optionality changes posture. When you negotiate from a position of desperation, it shows. When you negotiate from a position of stability, that shows, too.

When you consider a career pivot while in survival mode, it feels risky. When you consider it with some margin, it feels promising.

Financial peace also means less friction in daily life.

Bills don't cause dread. Unexpected expenses don't derail the month. Conversations about money don't explode into arguments.

You still discuss strategy. You still review goals. But you do so from steadiness, not urgency.

CALM AT HOME

If you have a copilot—a spouse or partner—this shift is especially noticeable. When both of you understand the plan, know the numbers, and trust the system, money conversations become shorter, calmer, and less charged.

You're no longer debating survival. You're fine-tuning your trajectory. That changes the emotional temperature of a household.

Financial peace also provides perspective. Short-term noise becomes less persuasive when you understand long-term math. This is where many men experience something unexpected: relief.

Not the adrenaline of winning. Not the thrill of outperformance. Relief.

The relief of not constantly calculating, comparing, or second-guessing.

REDEFINING WHAT YOU NEED

In Chapter 8, we asked you to think about the straightforward question, "What does my life require?"

Financial peace arrives when your system reliably—not extravagantly or perfectly—funds that answer.

You don't need to be the wealthiest person in your peer group to feel secure. You need to know your base is covered.

You want stable housing, manageable transportation, consistent savings, and diversified investments.

When those foundations are in place, your mind relaxes. This is also where time shifts. You stop obsessing over, "When can I retire?" and start asking, "What kind of life am I building?"

Retirement becomes less about escape and more about timing. Work becomes a choice, not a life sentence. You approach projects differently. You tolerate less nonsense. And, you invest in relationships more intentionally.

Financial peace is not about withdrawing from life. It's about living it without constant background anxiety. And that's worth far more than flashy items.

SECTION 3: KEEP IT SIMPLE FOR LIFE

BEWARE COMPLEXITY CREEP

In Chapter 6, we talked about "lifestyle creep." Now we'll discuss its cousin, "complexity creep," a hidden risk to long-term financial success.

As accounts grow and knowledge expands, it's tempting to layer on sophistication. More accounts. More strategies. More tweaks. More monitoring. At this point, your portfolio needs its own personal assistant.

But complexity often increases stress without increasing outcome. Simplicity is not naïveté. It's strategic restraint.

A calm money life does not require daily dashboards. It requires periodic check-ins. Once or twice a year, you sit down and review: Has income changed? Has spending increased? Is the savings rate aligned with goals? Is the asset allocation still appropriate?

You adjust if necessary. Then you step away.

You don't need to optimize every quarter. You need to stay consistent across decades.

SIMPLICITY PROTECTS THE SYSTEM

Avoiding complexity creep also means resisting the urge to reinvent your system whenever new financial trends emerge. There will always be new products, new asset classes, and new "guaranteed" strategies.

Your filter is simple: Does this materially improve my long-term plan? If not, you let it pass.

You don't have to chase every innovation to benefit from progress. Broad market funds incorporate innovation automatically. Your diversified portfolio already owns thousands of companies that are adapting and evolving. You don't need to micromanage that evolution.

This is where humility returns as an asset. The market is larger than your insight. Staying diversified acknowledges that reality.

Over decades, simplicity wins because it's sustainable. The Moderately Motivated Man does not aim to be the most financially clever person in the room. He aims to be the most consistent.

Consistency is easier when the system is understandable. If you can't explain your financial setup in a few sentences, it may be too complicated. You're running a household, not a Swiss bank.

Simplicity also helps your copilot. If something happens to you, could your partner understand and manage the system without a forensic accountant?

Clarity is a gift to your future self, and to anyone who might one day need to step in.

SERENITY NOW

At some point, you may look back and realize that the most powerful decisions were not dramatic or complicated. They were repetitive.

If you've followed the arc of this book—from reducing vagueness, to building clarity, to designing systems, to protecting against self-sabotage, to planning long term—you already have the pieces.

Now it's about maintenance, a simple rhythm like taking care of your lawn.

A brief annual review. A conversation with your copilot. A minor adjustment. A recommitment to simplicity. Then back to living.

You are no longer chasing a number. You are sustaining a system that offers you something priceless: calm.

Not the absence of uncertainty. But the presence of confidence.

And if you think back to where we started, this was never really about maximizing wealth. It was about reducing weight.

At the beginning of this book, money felt heavy. Heavy because it was vague. Heavy because it was uncertain. Heavy because you weren't sure whether one bad month could knock everything sideways.

But clarity removes uncertainty. Structure reduces fear. Margin gives you breathing room. And repetition builds confidence.

When money is understood, automated, diversified, and aligned with your version of *enough*, it becomes lighter.

And when money feels lighter, you feel lighter. You make decisions from a sense of steadiness rather than fear. You plan from confidence instead of urgency. You stop avoiding statements because you know where you stand.

When money runs quietly in the background, like plumbing or electricity, you don't think about it much.

Money no longer feels heavy. Life feels lighter. And you're free to live it the way you want.

KEY TAKEAWAYS FROM CHAPTER 10

1. *When Money Stops Dominating.* A calm money life emerges when income has a plan, spending is aligned, investing is automated, and risk is managed. Money shifts from a daily stressor to a steady foundation.
2. *What Financial Peace Feels Like.* Financial peace is flexibility, not luxury. Optionality reduces fear, lowers household tension, and replaces adrenaline with relief.
3. *Keep It Simple for Life.* Complexity adds stress without necessarily improving outcomes. Regular review, disciplined restraint, and sustainable systems protect calm over decades.

ACKNOWLEDGMENTS

The closing focus on simplicity and resisting "complexity creep" reflects a broader essentialist philosophy popularized by writers such as Greg McKeown, whose work highlights the power of doing fewer things better. It also aligns with the low-drama investing approach articulated in J.L.

Collins' *The Simple Path to Wealth*, which reinforces the idea that understandable, repeatable systems tend to outperform constant optimization over time.

MODERATELY PAINLESS EXERCISE

A CALM MONEY DAY

After everything you've built in this book—visibility, margin, automation, simplicity, and restraint—what does the result feel like? Let's define it.

Step 1: Describe a Calm Money Day

Complete this sentence: "On a calm money day, I _____."

Examples:

- Don't think about my accounts at all.
- Check balances without anxiety.
- Spend within my plan without second-guessing.
- Know that bills are paid automatically.
- Feel confident during market swings.
- Focus on work, family, or hobbies instead of numbers.

Write 3–5 short lines that complete the sentence. Not aspirations. Descriptions. What does steady look like?

Step 2: Identify What Makes It Possible

Now write another sentence: "A calm money day is possible because ____."

Examples:

- I know my burn rate.
- I have a buffer.
- My investments are automated.
- I've defined *enough*.
- I don't react to headlines.

Step 3: Keep It Visible

Save what you wrote somewhere accessible. Not as motivation. As perspective.

When money feels heavy again, and it occasionally will, re-read your answers. The goal is lighter living.

A calm money life doesn't mean you ignore money. It means your money system is working, and you're free to live your life.

CONCLUSION

FROM UNDERSTANDING TO ACTION

If you're reading this, you made it to the end. That alone is worth acknowledging.

Most men wouldn't read an entire book about money. They'd skim headlines. Collect tips. Absorb fragments. But you stayed with it. You wrestled with the uncomfortable parts. You replaced uncertainty with clarity.

And you now understand more than you did when you began.

You understand why money felt heavy. How margin reduces fragility. Why simplicity beats complexity. How consistency compounds.

More importantly, you understand how to think about money. That shift matters.

Once you understand how it works, money stops feeling mysterious. It stops feeling like a secret code everyone else somehow cracked. It becomes a practical system—one that can be built, maintained, and trusted.

The natural next question is, "What do I do next?"

The answer is straightforward. You implement calmly.

THE NEXT MEASURED STEP

You don't need to become a portfolio technician. You don't need to engineer your own financial infrastructure. The tools already exist.

Established, low-cost firms (such as Vanguard, Fidelity, and Schwab) have built platforms designed for long-term, diversified investors. Their systems make it easy to open accounts, select broad index funds, and automate contributions.

If you prefer guidance, a fee-only fiduciary advisor can help translate these principles into a simple plan.

You are not outsourcing responsibility. You are outsourcing the plumbing.

Your mission is not to outsmart the market. Your job is to connect to the right tools that reward steadiness.

Open the account. Choose the diversified, low-cost option. Set up the automatic transfer. Then let repetition take over. And get out of the way.

You now know enough to recognize hype and avoid unnecessary complexity. You know to ask better questions and stay away from drama.

This knowledge reduces anxiety.

BUILD IT. THEN LET IT RUN.

From here forward, money should move from being a mysterious project to being a simple system. Projects demand constant tinkering. Systems only need regular review.

Make adjustments if needed. Then step away.

The world will remain loud. Markets will swing. Someone will always have a story about a quick gain. But you don't need to chase stories.

You have structure.

Over time, that structure becomes quiet confidence. Every year won't be smooth, but you'll understand what's happening. You'll expect cycles. Because you've built for them.

When your money is organized and automated, it stops taking up mental space. Money becomes a framework, one that is functional, reliable, and supportive. That's the point: A system that works without demanding your attention every day.

From here, your responsibilities are simple: Maintain the rhythm. Contribute. Review occasionally. Adjust lightly. Continue.

Years from now, you may not remember the exact numbers you started with. But you will remember that you chose steadiness over drama. And that choice compounds.

You don't need to conquer money. You don't need to impress anyone with it. You simply need to keep it organized, automated, and aligned with your version of *enough*.

You made it to the end of this book. That means you care about getting this right. Now you have the tools to do it.

Take the next measured step. Set up your system. Let it run.

And then get back to living.

ABOUT THE AUTHOR

Rick Resnick is a former newspaper writer, magazine publisher, and longtime media executive whose byline has appeared in sponsored features across *Fortune, TIME, People,* and *Sports Illustrated,* among others.

Rick isn't a Wall Street insider or a financial guru—though a decade working at *Money* magazine taught him a thing or two about keeping finances simple. His own financial "a-ha" moment came while reading *The Wealthy Barber* and discovering the benefits of living below your means, investing consistently, keeping costs low, and letting compounding do its quiet magic.

Through *The Moderately Motivated Man* series, Rick writes practical, accessible self-help for guys who want to build better lives without added stress, hustle culture, or personality overhauls. This money guide follows *The Moderately Motivated Man's Guide to Time Management* and *The Moderately Motivated Man's Guide to Habits*, continuing the mission of helping men get better at life—without trying too hard.

When he's not writing, Rick plays tennis and golf, obsessively supports Arsenal FC, and sings lead in a rock cover band based in Pike County, Pennsylvania. He still checks his investment accounts occasionally—but not obsessively and rarely after a market dip. The less drama, the better.

THANK YOU FOR READING

You made it to the last page. Now you can calmly take charge of your finances—without turning money into a full-time job.

One small favor: If this book helped you, a short review on your favorite book site can help other Moderately Motivated Men discover it. A few sentences mean more than you might think.

Scan the code or visit:

MoneyReview.ModeratelyMotivatedMan.com

For updates on future books, join the MMM mailing list:

signup.ModeratelyMotivatedMan.com

And if you know someone who feels stressed, overwhelmed, or intimidated by money, consider telling him about this book.

With appreciation—Rick Resnick

contact.ModeratelyMotivatedMan.com

www.ingramcontent.com/pod-product-compliance
Lightning Source LLC
LaVergne TN
LVHW100732061126
851857LV00011B/500
9798991242981